READY FOR THE
Workforce

ENGAGING STRATEGIES FOR TEACHING SECONDARY LEARNERS EMPLOYABILITY SKILLS

CHRISTI McBRIDE   BRENDA DUNCAN-DAVIS

Solution Tree | Press

a division of
Solution Tree

555 North Morton Street
Bloomington, IN 47404
800.733.6786 (toll free) / 812.336.7700
FAX: 812.336.7790

email: info@SolutionTree.com
SolutionTree.com

Visit **go.SolutionTree.com/21stcenturyskills** to download the free reproducibles in this book.

Printed in the United States of America

Library of Congress Cataloging-in-Publication Data

Names: McBride, Christi, author. | Duncan-Davis, Brenda, author.
Title: Ready for the workforce : engaging strategies for teaching secondary
   learners employability skills / Christi McBride, Brenda Duncan-Davis.
Description: Bloomington, IN : Solution Tree Press, [2021] | Includes
   bibliographical references and index.
Identifiers: LCCN 2020035081 (print) | LCCN 2020035082 (ebook) | ISBN
   9781949539790 (paperback) | ISBN 9781949539806 (ebook)
Subjects: LCSH: Career education--United States. | Employability--Study and
   teaching--United States.
Classification: LCC LC1037.5 .M394 2021 (print) | LCC LC1037.5 (ebook) |
   DDC 370.1130973--dc23
LC record available at https://lccn.loc.gov/2020035081
LC ebook record available at https://lccn.loc.gov/2020035082

Solution Tree
Jeffrey C. Jones, CEO
Edmund M. Ackerman, President

Solution Tree Press
President and Publisher: Douglas M. Rife
Associate Publisher: Sarah Payne-Mills
Art Director: Rian Anderson
Managing Production Editor: Kendra Slayton
Copy Chief: Jessi Finn
Production Editor: Rita Carlberg
Content Development Specialist: Amy Rubenstein
Proofreader: Kate St. Ives
Text and Cover Designer: Laura Cox
Editorial Assistants: Sarah Ludwig and Elijah Oates

Acknowledgments

We want to express our thanks to our friends and loved ones for their contributions to the development of our employability-skills framework. Thank you to our industry partners who shared their workforce needs with us; our families, who often heard us say, "We're going to be busy working on the book"; and the supporting team at Solution Tree, who believed in our vision. We are extremely grateful to have had all of you support us throughout this process.

We knew that these ideas needed to come to life and that students would benefit greatly once the book was completed. We truly cannot put into words the gratitude that we have for the curriculum specialists who researched and wrote the lessons for the employability-skills curriculum that are in this book. These curriculum specialists were the boots on the ground, creating and practicing in the field. Special recognition goes to the following people, whom we've listed alongside the core topics on which they worked and the state standards to which they adhered in order to help create and add richness to the employability-skills curriculum.

- Londa Hight (career-pathway preparation, teamwork, and problem solving, as well as our chapter on growth mindset, resilience, and grit)

- Kristen Portteus (communication, diversity, and time management)

- Andrea Smith (résumés, employer panels, mock interviews, first impressions, and alignment of Indiana English language arts standards)

- Megan Brown (resource allocation, decision making, and integrity)

- Derek Morgan (teamwork challenges)

- Ella Padula (alignment of Indiana social studies standards)

- Diane Rodriquez (alignment of Indiana mathematics standards)

Solution Tree Press would like to thank the following reviewers:

Erica Ajayi
Interim Principal
John Marshall Mid-High
  Enterprise School
Oklahoma City, Oklahoma

Jay Clark
Principal
Van Buren Middle School
Van Buren, Ohio

Antonio DeMelo
Principal
East Granby High School
East Granby, Connecticut

Alison Douglas
Career and Technical Education Teacher
Arlington High School
Arlington, Washington

Margo Fraczek
Principal
Coakley Middle School
Norwood, Massachusetts

Darin Johnston
Sixth-Grade Teacher
North Fayette Valley Middle School
Elgin, Iowa

Jed Kees
Principal
Onalaska Middle School
Onalaska, Wisconsin

Jeffrey Koenig
District Administrator
Stanley-Boyd Area Schools
Stanley, Wisconsin

Erin Kowalik
Biology Teacher
James Bowie High School
Austin, Texas

Louis Lim
Vice Principal
Richmond Green Secondary School
Richmond Hill, Ontario, Canada

Josh Lyons
Director of Teaching and Learning
Solon Community School District
Solon, Iowa

Tanya Mahr
Principal
Stanley-Boyd Area Schools
Stanley, Wisconsin

Lindsey Matkin
Assistant Principal
Preston Middle School
Fort Collins, Colorado

Brett McCann
Principal
Willowick Middle School
Willowick, Ohio

Randall Peterson
Assistant Professor
Barry University
Miami Shores, Florida

Visit **go.SolutionTree.com/21stcenturyskills** to
download the free reproducibles in this book.

Table of Contents

About the Authors

**Christi McBride** serves as director of Hoosier Hills Career Center in Bloomington, Indiana. She began her career in education as an elementary counselor and then moved into the high school setting as a guidance director. Her current position in secondary administration, specifically as a regional career and technical education director, has proven to be rewarding beyond measure. Christi has presented at conferences across multiple states and offered on-site professional development for local and international leaders, including the Mandela Washington Fellowship. Her focus on working with students, school staff, and community partners to provide positive, productive outcomes for all students led to the Youth Employability Skills, or YES!, curriculum, which she developed with her colleague Brenda Duncan-Davis and a talented group of curriculum specialists dedicated to engaging and empowering students.

Christi is an active member of the Indiana Association for Career and Technical Education (ACTE) and in 2015 received the Indiana ACTE Administrator of the Year award. In 2018, the Greater Bloomington Chamber of Commerce honored her with a Women Excel Bloomington Award for her leadership in the educational and business community. Her students and teachers nominated her for the Family, Career and Community Leaders of America's Administrator of the Year, a designation she received in 2020. Christi is also a longtime member of the Indiana Counseling Association (ICA), receiving its Award for Leadership and Service in 1995 as a new counselor. She served on the ICA governing board and conference committee for multiple years.

Christi received her bachelor's and master's degrees from Indiana University Bloomington. She received her license in educational leadership from Indiana State University and continues her own professional development with Purdue University's leadership development program, which she has attended and presented at since 2014.

Brenda Duncan-Davis is an educational consultant specializing in bridging education and industry through the facilitation of work-based learning opportunities, registered apprenticeship programs, and professional development in workplace-readiness skills. As a career and technical educator and work-based learning coordinator, she created an internship program, a service-learning course, and education-pathway field experiences. Brenda is an avid grant writer, helping to fund classroom projects, community outreach endeavors, and postgraduation career development programs. Her background in work-based learning led to the development of the YES! curriculum with her colleague Christi McBride and a wonderful team of curriculum specialists.

Brenda is a member of the American Association of Family and Consumer Sciences (AAFCS), holding different leadership roles at local and state levels. She was a charter member of the Delta Kappa Gamma Society's Gamma Nu Chapter and served on Ivy Tech Community College Bloomington's Education Advisory Board. She has received the Indiana Department of Education's Learn and Serve Educator Award, as well as recognitions such as the AAFCS's Indiana Affiliate Teacher of the Year, the AAFCS's National Teacher of Merit, and the Indiana Association of Career and Technical Education's Outstanding Teacher of the Year. In 2016, she received the Indiana Association of Career and Technical Education's Lifetime Achievement Award.

Brenda has presented at state and national conferences on service-learning and employability skills. She contributed to the book *Shifting Gears: Alert Today, Alive Tomorrow* and *Ignite* magazine—student-produced works that promote safe teen driving. In 2016, she cowrote *Capturing Memories: Articles, Interviews and Timelines of Owen County, Indiana*, with an English teacher, who was a former student.

Brenda completed her education at Indiana University, receiving a bachelor of science in vocational home economics and a master of arts in teaching with a concentration in vocational education.

To book Christi McBride or Brenda Duncan-Davis for professional development, contact pd@SolutionTree.com.

Preface

We truly love our students. The two of us have spent our entire careers, sixty-eight years collectively, as high school educators working to enrich students' lives in whatever way possible. But what does that mean, really? We bring students clothing to wear during interviews, send them home with food for the weekend, and support them emotionally when times are tough. We do our best to unconditionally care for *the whole student*. It was a natural step for us to create a curriculum that would provide students with skills they need to confidently enter the workforce.

To determine what would be key in training students for their future workplaces, we spent months meeting with numerous industry partners to pinpoint the skills that would positively impact workforce development. In addition to researching what was stated on a national level, we felt it important to collect information that reflected local perspectives, so we organized an open forum with more than twenty-five south-central Indiana employers situated within industries such as life science, advanced manufacturing, health science, postsecondary education, economic development, and commercial building construction. We asked that they answer the simple question, "What qualities are you looking for in an employee?" Common responses included the distinct abilities to learn tasks, be respectful of other people and one's environment, communicate effectively, and actively solve problems. For us, this local survey of essential skills became our compass, with both state and national lists of essential skills validating these skill sets. We wanted to not just go on our gut reactions to employers' needs but vet and evaluate them alongside the Indiana Department of Workforce Development's Employability Skills Benchmarks and the Office of Career, Technical, and Adult Education's Employability Skills Framework. The skills that state and national agencies found to be essential reflected those that local industry partners cited. Using this input from local employers, as well as state and national data, we came up with core employability skills to develop into a teaching curriculum.

Once we agreed on the core skills, we gathered multiple experts together and began developing strategies and activities through which we would engage and empower students to gain these skills. Our initial curriculum format included sixteen core lessons that varied in duration and could be integrated across multiple subject areas. We launched the curriculum in schools across twelve counties and garnered positive feedback, which led to our receiving professional development training requests and offering both state and national presentations on the curriculum. These growing opportunities prompted us to write this book as a way to help other educators—resulting in a framework of nine skill sets that teachers can embed in their existing curricula.

Whether students' postsecondary plan is to pursue further education, join the military, or seek direct workforce placement, in our view, all learners are pursuing career goals requiring specific skills. According to the U.S. Department of Education's Office of Career, Technical, and Adult Education (2016), "Employability skills, along with academic and technical skills, are an essential component of college and career readiness." Our work with learning targets around identified employability-skill components began simply from a need to provide, in an intentional manner, employability skills to students preparing to exit the high school setting. Creating a curriculum crosswalked with multiple academic standards provided a comprehensive skill alignment for workforce development. To ensure we truly reached all students and adhered to the Every Student Succeeds Act (ESSA, 2015) and the Strengthening Career and Technical Education for the 21st Century Act (2018), also known as *Perkins V*, we built a framework using a universal design for learning methodology that would provide educators with the ability to establish employable workers. This framework included activities for all students because offering a continuum of training modalities for students of all learning levels is critical to successfully incorporating employability skills into classroom instruction.

In order to determine the feasibility and effectiveness of what we termed our Youth Employability Skills, or YES!, framework, we initiated a pilot effort first at our school, Hoosier Hills Career Center, and then at four comprehensive high schools, where our curriculum specialists tried out their lessons and others. Next, we presented to sixteen Indiana school systems, who then began using the framework. Participating teachers confirmed the ease of integrating the framework's activities into their existing curricular content and reported strong student engagement. Industry partners' input confirmed that our approach to teaching vital standards had indeed transformed into a powerful program of acquired skills. Our melding of education and industry had led to focused research, which had given life to the framework that we have shared with students and are now so delighted to share with you. We hope you find this framework as engaging and empowering as they have.

Introduction

Why have we written a book about the importance of teaching employability skills to students? First, so teachers can assist students in developing valuable skills for their futures; second, so teachers can help meet industry needs for a qualified workforce; and last, so schools can be in accordance with the U.S. Department of Education's legislative mandates. But what undergirds these straightforward objectives is our real passion to ultimately make students' and teachers' lives richer and easier to navigate through practical means. In preparation for this, we'd like to discuss the nature of employability skills, review some of the educational initiatives and workforce programs that demonstrate the relevance of employability skills, outline the framework we developed, identify who will benefit from the book, and explore the book's basic structure.

Employability Skills Explained

What are employability skills? They are the essential abilities or competencies necessary for an individual to be a dynamic, thriving member of the global workplace. Employers often talk about *soft skills* or *professional skills* as being those attributes that make a person a good employee. These interchangeable terms describe the same set of skills as employability skills—and as educators, we need to listen to what businesses and organizations need because our ultimate goal is to give our students the tools for them to succeed in their postgraduation lives.

Employability skills are becoming more important than academic and technical skills when it comes to success in the workforce. Jennifer Radin, Steve Hatfield, Jeff Schwartz, and Colleen Bordeaux (2020) of Deloitte write that "now, possibly more than ever, there appears to be an impetus for employees to bring their 'soft' skills—such as creativity, leadership, and critical thinking—to work." "Wait a minute," you might say. "Do you mean employability skills have more relevance to professional success than the required academic or technical skills of a job do?" The hard truth is yes. Often, we hear employers state they can train any individual who has the willingness to learn but they cannot teach someone work ethic. Employers tell us that their companies can offer incentives, sign-on bonuses, and other reward systems to encourage current and potential employees but that, really, employees must be eager to meet employers' expectations in order to succeed. That is why your role as an educator is of utmost importance. For you, the educator, the framework we outline in this book provides a step forward in building students' workplace competence, which will entail embedding essential employability skills into your established curriculum—discussing the skills as they relate to a given content area and associated technical skills, as well as setting up classroom activities on these skills.

The Impetus for Our Work: Educational Initiatives and Workforce Programs

Those entering and transitioning into the workforce often lack the professional skills necessary to compete for entry-level or middle-skill positions. But there are federal, state, and local opportunities available, including educational initiatives and workforce development programs, that encourage educators and business leaders to connect youths and adults with relevant training in employability skill sets. These existing educational initiatives and workforce development programs give us a foundation for understanding employability skills and their relevance.

In the United States, the objective to empower educators and their students with college- and career-readiness plans and measures came to a head with the federal legislation known as the Every Student Succeeds Act (ESSA, 2015). Signed into law in 2015, ESSA mandates state and local public education agencies to educate and prepare all K–12 students to succeed in college and during their careers. ESSA requires education to align to business and industry needs for in-demand jobs by integrating employment content into rigorous academic standards. All fifty states are required to attend to ESSA guidelines for high school diplomas, according to the 2018 federal ruling (U.S. Department of Education, n.d.). Individual state requirements centered on workforce initiatives such as employability-skills training are forthcoming as workforce-alignment initiatives increase. In addition, the U.S. Department of Education's Office of Career, Technical, and Adult Education; several industry partners; and federal agencies created the national employability-skills framework as a guide for increasing college and career readiness (Office of Career, Technical, and Adult Education, 2016).

You may already be familiar with the Strengthening Career and Technical Education for the 21st Century Act (2018), also referred to as *Perkins V.* This act was passed to support educators in more fully nurturing academic rigor, technical knowledge, and employability skills in all secondary students and postsecondary students enrolled in career and technical education (CTE) programs. As with ESSA, the goal of Perkins V is to prepare all students for further education and for careers in current or emerging professions—in high-skill, high-wage, or in-demand occupations. Perkins V emphasizes *all* students by increasing employment opportunities for specific populations—including students with disabilities, those who are economically disadvantaged, and those in foster care or facing homelessness.

As federal programs, Perkins V and ESSA require all states to implement employability skills as well as college- and career-readiness content yet grant flexible means for educators to adhere to these mandates. Let's take a brief look at how a few U.S. states and organizations are responding to the need for solid workforce-pipeline development through employability-skills instruction.

Georgia is a leader in educational initiatives regarding career preparation and employability skills. Georgia was the first state to require all high school students to have a career pathway and in 2019 launched the International Skills Diploma Seal to signify workplace readiness (Georgia Department of Education, 2016, 2019). Georgia's career, technical, and agricultural education (CTAE) program recognizes pathway skills, leadership skills, and employability skills (Mann, 2018). From the work of the Georgia Employability Skills Task Force and other stakeholders, Georgia has identified four workforce-building priorities, with one centered on teaching employability skills throughout grades K–12 (Georgia Department of Education, 2019). These intentional opportunities for instruction center, in part, on developing a workforce with the explicit direction of industry needs, and they help nurture long-term, career-focused employees.

Wisconsin is known for having high-quality career centers, which offer multiple apprenticeship programs. In Wisconsin, work-based learning is encouraged for students to gain employability and occupational skills. The state's goal to reinforce the connection between work and school improves students' employment options and helps solidify their career interests. Students can earn a state-credentialed Youth Leadership and Employability Skills Certificate, which indicates they have acquired transferable skills and proven themselves career ready (Wisconsin Department of Public Instruction, 2015).

State industries, along with education, are identifying the need to upskill their current workforce and striving to meet ever-changing requirements. The Minnesota Job Skills Partnership, administered by the Minnesota Department of Employment and Economic Development (2019), offers grants to support workforce development.

This partnership program allows business and education to work together to develop cooperative training for new or incumbent workers, tailoring the training to specific business needs. Also, the Minnesota Job Skills Partnership's Pathways Program focuses on providing new job and career pathways for individuals who are living below federal poverty guidelines or who are making the transition from public assistance to the workforce.

Skillful (2018), a nonprofit employee development initiative from the Markle Foundation, originated in Colorado in 2015 and then expanded to Indiana in 2018. Sponsored by Microsoft, Walmart, and the Lumina Foundation, Skillful aims to enable all Americans to obtain employment in an ever-changing economy. It works with employers to recruit and hire based on required skills, rather than on traditional educational prerequisites. It promotes using skills-based job postings to increase the talent pool and find the best potential candidates. Skillful also offers career-coaching training so that career coaches in workforce centers, secondary and postsecondary institutions, and nonprofit groups can better help individuals explore career options and create skills-based résumés. It uses this skills-based hiring methodology to address workforce development efforts (Skillful, 2018).

Data are important when evaluating initiatives; however, more important is the initiatives' personal impact on students and employees and their long-term quality of life. Living in a state with clearly defined expectations for employability skills and seeing those expectations' impact on young people transitioning into careers validates the importance of college and career readiness. And in keeping with the legislative requirements this book helps meet, we absolutely believe in teaching employability skills to *all* students. Often, educators hear that college is not for everyone and we need to be preparing non-college-bound students to enter the workforce immediately after graduation. Our philosophy is to prepare all students, learners at all levels, for their future, which will include a career. We want students to each reach their highest potential and be fully prepared for advancement opportunities. Our overall goal is to equip all students with skills that will be beneficial as they navigate their individual life courses.

Our Employability-Skills Framework

Our Youth Employability Skills, or YES!, framework provides students an opportunity to learn and cultivate the skills employers expect them to demonstrate—the essential attributes for success in the workplace. We created this framework to better meet the needs of our students and the business community. We enlisted the help of curriculum specialists to work alongside us as we researched a multitude of resources and instructional strategies and developed sixteen core topics around which educators could teach employability skills to middle and high school students. Initially, the curriculum activities we developed, ranging from a single session to a weeklong unit, covered the areas of resource allocation, career-pathway preparation, communication, critical thinking, decision making, diversity, effective workplace relationships, employer panels, first impressions, integrity, mock interviews, problem solving, résumés, teamwork, teamwork challenges, and time management. With these sixteen core topics serving as its foundation, the framework evolved into a collection of the nine skills around which this book is based. These nine essential skills for success are as follows.

1. Communication: Arguably the most foundational skill, communication involves sending and receiving information verbally and nonverbally, and in the workplace, it requires an ability to understand and validate diverse viewpoints among colleagues.

2. Teamwork and collaboration: Teamwork occurs when a group of people come together to make strides toward a shared outcome or solution. A productive team works to understand the ideas and abilities unique to each member and of the whole group. As a part of the collective, one must share ideas cooperatively and consider other members' contributions, which leads to successful collaboration.

3. Critical thinking and problem solving: With this skill set, one must demonstrate an ability to think deeply and creatively through challenging situations and, as a result, make sound decisions.

4. Workplace relationship building: Developing adaptability, taking initiative, and embracing diversity assist in sustaining effective relationships in general, and likewise these skills are critical in the workplace.

5. Resource management: This skill requires a person to be reliable and nimble and to respond punctually to project necessities. Employees with resource-management skills understand the key elements of a high-performing work group and agree to active participation and accountability.

6. Growth mindset, resilience, and grit: A growth mindset is a frame of mind or a belief system used to process incoming information and navigate challenges. A person needs resilience and grit when sustained effort is required to move forward when unexpected setbacks crop up.

7. Ethics, values, and integrity: This skill set includes the ability to demonstrate ethical behavior and maintain high expectations for oneself—skills positively regarded in any workplace. Conducting oneself in an honest manner creates a desirable candidate for employment.

8. Networking and interview know-how: This denotes the ability to communicate or interact with others to develop social connections and to take that expertise into a discussion on career topics.

9. Career-pathway preparation: This refers to a career awareness and readiness that encompasses one's interests, skills, and work ethic, creating a comprehensive means for carving out a suitable career path.

Our placing this framework in the hands of educators confirmed the validity and documented the success of our work. To give you an idea of the depth and breadth of our YES! outreach, we shared the framework with eighty-one school corporations, eighteen career centers, three charter schools, three private high schools, two special education cooperatives, seven Department of Correction facilities, and four colleges and universities, representing fifty-eight Indiana counties. Positive feedback from these entities led to our presenting at multiple conferences, expanding the use of this framework into an additional eight U.S. states and eighteen countries across Africa, and ultimately writing this book—with the hope that others will apply the knowledge and tools herein.

Whether students transition to a career after high school or after postsecondary education or training, all students need this framework's skills in workforce readiness. The framework addresses college and career readiness and offers practitioners a comprehensive program in an easy-to-use format that includes content knowledge, instructional strategies, and resources. Our employability-skills framework also provides teacher-friendly activities designed to engage students while they interact with the essential skills.

Our framework embeds easily into any school's current courses, and practitioners can determine the best implementation method for their students to get the maximum benefit. We have observed schools using the framework in courses teaching career awareness, career preparation, competencies, and life skills. Other schools have used the framework during advisory periods and homeroom to provide support for students' social and emotional learning. School counselors and career coaches may find the book's content valuable in working with small groups in classrooms or as a pullout program. Another delivery method could include faculty members reviewing content to determine crossover standards for various subjects. The faculty members would then embed employability-skills topics into those lessons and share with the rest of the school staff as part of professional development. We know that educators already have a lot on their plates, so whether you incorporate the topics into a CTE program, Jobs for America's Graduates (JAG), or academic and elective courses, the framework offers you practical strategies for engaging students in skill development.

The employability-skills framework provides a tool for practitioners to connect students with a panorama of possibilities and a vision for the future, while concurrently establishing a talent pipeline for the workforce. In development, we focused on engaging teachers, counselors, homeroom advisers, youth workers, and, most important, students in an empowering process that builds a common language for essential employability skills. Through this book, all practitioners who serve and educate students globally can gain an understanding of their role in connecting learners at all levels with the necessary skills to effectively prepare for the workforce.

Who This Book Benefits

This book's content crosses disciplines and can be used in a multitude of courses, ranging from English to a skilled trade. All practitioners, including teachers, counselors, advisers, and administrators who are part of public, private, or parochial school settings in grades 6–12 and postsecondary institutions will find this book of use in developing employability-skills lessons. If you want to make a difference in the lives of your students as they progress and transition into adulthood, then read this book and incorporate its concepts. It is that simple. The skills we identify and the accompanying activities will transform your instruction and make for confident, well-rounded, career-ready students.

About the Book's Structure

Each chapter outlines one of the nine essential skills for success. Chapter 1 explores the foundational skill of effective written, verbal, and nonverbal communication, which students will need for all workplace interactions and which will strengthen the remaining employability skills. In chapter 2, we'll take a closer look at teamwork and collaboration, a skill set that promotes belonging and, in the workplace, allows employees to work toward shared goals. Chapter 3, on critical thinking and problem solving, introduces the essential, though often difficult to pin down, skill set that will translate to creative, thoughtful approaches to workplace tasks. Chapter 4 covers how to assist your students in developing effective workplace relationships characterized by respect, appreciation of diversity, and openness to others' opinions and perspectives, which lead to enriched, reasoned outcomes on the job. Chapter 5, on resource management, details how you can help students make the most of their knowledge, skills, and time and connect with community organizations and agencies—promoting adaptability, accountability, and civic engagement. Chapter 6 builds on adaptability, explaining the significance of a growth mindset, resilience, and grit, which will allow students to not only see challenges as learning opportunities but recognize that their personal growth is limitless, setting them up to work toward their dreams and feel confident in the workplace. Chapter 7 explores ethics, values, and integrity, a skill set associated with one's moral compass, compatibility with a company's mission, and ability to adhere to safety protocols and best practices. Chapter 8 dives into networking and interview know-how, a skill set that will impact students' very livelihoods, ensuring that they understand how best to conduct themselves in professional situations. Finally, chapter 9 discusses career-pathway preparation, a skill set you can foster in students so that they gain self-awareness of their aptitudes, personality traits, and interests and begin to research their ideal careers.

In each of these skills chapters, you'll find three primary sections: (1) Rationale, (2) Research, and (3) Relay. The Rationale section provides logical reasoning behind the skill's inclusion, along with a broad perspective and oftentimes a real-life student example—the most powerful reason to embed the skill's development into your classroom practice. The Research section offers evidence from education and industry that supports the skill's relevance, and data that reflect research at national, state, and local levels. Finally, the Relay section is the point at which we hand the baton to you, and you integrate the skill or skill set into your established curriculum through strategies and activities that will allow students to master the given topic. Throughout each chapter, we'll include scenarios from our professional experiences to shed light on the influence that employability-skills training has on students, school staff, and even industry partners.

To ensure the validity of the YES! program, we developed and included in the appendix (see page 123) a crosswalk that aligns the Indiana Department of Education's academic standards for the courses Preparing for College and Careers, Cooperative Education, and CTE: Work-Based Learning; the JAG competencies; the Indiana Department of Workforce Development's Employability Skills Benchmarks; and the Office of Career, Technical, and Adult Education's Employability Skills Framework. The comprehensive crosswalk demonstrates the intentional connection of multiple standards within our employability-skills framework.

The activities you'll find in this book provide students opportunities to practice the identified skill sets *without fear of failure*. These strategies allow for participation and connection in a nonthreatening fashion, rather than a pass-fail or a letter grade to denote how well a student performs. Students continuously engage in a cycle of usage with each employability skill. Practicing the skill provides necessary repetition, which leads to positive habitual behavior and ingrained concepts for all students. Becoming proficient with these skills will not only equip all students for the careers of their choosing but will help them develop greater self-awareness; confidence; and a deeper, richer understanding of the people and the world around them. What more could we want for our 21st century learners?

CHAPTER 1

Communication

Communication—verbal and nonverbal—serves as the foundation of the employability-skills framework. So much is involved in communication within education and the workplace. For example, after an opportunity we had to teach the communication activities presented in this chapter, we were stopped in our tracks by the remarkable conversations that took place among our students. The students readily demonstrated a variety of communication skills. They were able to contribute enlightened solutions to the problems we presented to them, collaborate with group members, and clearly share the critical content covered in each activity. Through the interactive instructional strategies within the classroom lesson, students were able to tackle the appropriate, effective communication that is essential for positive interactions in the workplace.

Communication has a connection to almost all other professional skills. This chapter will offer ways to address various aspects of communication through the lens of the employability-skills framework. As you think through your use of the framework, consider how you might engage your students in an examination of a wide variety of communication skills. For example, written language skills clearly translate to use in the workplace, whereas social media usage and body language may not be as obvious to students in their relation to professional communication among coworkers. But each aspect of communication plays a significant role in workplace relationships and takes practice to navigate with success. Let's take a look at the rationale behind nurturing communication skills in students, the research that illustrates communication skills' relevance in the workforce, and activities that will help facilitate this skill development in students.

Rationale

We had the opportunity to talk with a vice president of marketing for a local industry partner of ours who was struggling to hire an intern for his department. Let us call our vice president friend Bruce. During our discussion, after we mentioned that our school, a career and technical education center, teaches students résumé writing, we asked Bruce to review a few samples of student résumés and offer structural feedback as part of our advisory board for the center. Bruce stopped us midsentence and said, "You mean to tell me that your high school students all have résumés?" He was sincerely stunned that high school–aged students had completed résumés as part of an employability-skills lesson. Then, Bruce shared what he had experienced with several non-résumé-holding college students he'd recently interviewed. These intern candidates from a local university had not only come to their interviews without résumés, and without business cards that linked to digital résumés or portfolios, but they'd had difficulty responding to what Bruce considered basic, straightforward questions. He'd wondered, "How could this be possible?" The college students had numerous opportunities to attend résumé-writing sessions provided through the university's placement office. Bruce was shocked that this occurred; he could not believe these theoretically career-ready college juniors and seniors were not prepared to enter an interview with developed résumés and composed interpersonal communication skills.

The scenario Bruce presented drove home for us that middle and high school teachers must teach their students effective communication skills through not only essay writing, for example, but verbal interactions. Though testing, by nature, requires a focus on written communication skills, instruction for students needs to go far beyond such testing requirements. Before students leave high school, teachers must discuss with them how to effectively communicate so that students understand the various forms of communication necessary to transition from school to work.

Research

Effective communication—written, verbal, and nonverbal—is a critical employability skill. When Hart Research Associates (2013) conducted a survey of 318 employers, 93 percent of respondents agreed that "a candidate's demonstrated capacity to think critically, *communicate clearly*, and solve complex problems is more important than their undergraduate major" (emphasis added). Similarly, the Association for Career and Technical Education's (2018) fact sheet of skills that employers desire highlights oral communication and written communication as two of the five most important aptitudes.

According to Concordia University, St. Paul (2017), the workplace demands that people use interpersonal, verbal, and nonverbal communication effectively, appropriately, and respectfully. As educators, we need to make sure our students can write clearly, convey ideas and information thoughtfully and concisely, and listen to and appreciate other people's perspectives. While these communication skills are essential in the classroom and highly valued in the workplace, hiring managers across the board share concerns that a growing number of employees are deficient in this arena. Staffing company Adecco (2020) conducted a survey of employers in which 44 percent of executives stated that the U.S. workforce lacks "critical soft skills such as communication."

Issues surrounding this skill extend beyond the United States. The Australian Government (n.d.) has been working on the country's skills gap since the late 20th century, with its efforts resulting in the Core Skills for Work, which establishes performance indicators targeting employability skills. The Core Skills for Work framework highlights the importance of instructing youth and career seekers so they may become proficient workplace communicators—so they'll choose, for example, "appropriate communication protocols and conventions in a broad range of work contexts, with a growing awareness of the sometimes subtle impacts of choices made" (Australian Government, n.d.). Likewise, the framework addresses social etiquette around social media and cautions workers on the amount of time they spend creating a digital paper trail with the variety of content they browse and interact with over time (Australian Government, 2020).

In the same vein, the amount of screen time that students get and the amount of screen time they are expected to conform to are both rapidly increasing. Monica Anderson and Jingjing Jiang (2018) of the Pew Research Center find that 95 percent of U.S. teens have a smartphone or access to one, and 45 percent of thirteen- to seventeen-year-olds report being online on a constant basis. And according to professor James M. Lang (2020), "One survey of more than 3,000 parents found that screen time for their kids had increased by 500% during the [COVID-19] pandemic." Though parents and educators use technology as a means to connect students to learning opportunities, according to writer Kathryn Hulick (2020), online learning and students' regular use of Netflix, YouTube, and social media platforms present problems for students, hindering their ability to communicate effectively in person. But they may also struggle with capitalization, spelling, and etiquette when it comes to emailing in a professional setting. During the late 20th century, working solely from home was in its infancy; now, in the 21st century, technology-powered remote workspaces are ever growing and provide a wide variety of career choices for those entering the workforce. NPR's David Greene (as cited in Rosalsky, 2020) shares that an estimated 37 percent of work is possible to complete at home, yet prior to the COVID-19 pandemic, a mere 4 percent of Americans were actually working remotely. Businesses just like schools have learned to function in a flurry of online learning and video-conferencing modalities. All these trends reinforce the need for students to grasp all the differences between the shorthand and informalities among friends and the type of professional correspondence that employers are guaranteed to expect.

Digital communication is the new norm, resulting in fewer opportunities for students to hone their interpersonal communication skills. Because of this, practitioners must do more to instill workplace-readiness skills across the communication spectrum. They must have students practice and polish interpersonal skills through face-to-face interaction. Ironically, the COVID-19 pandemic's impact on traditional education methods has brought about changes in instruction among students and teachers in the area of interpersonal communication. School leader Aisha Bonner (as cited in Hulick, 2020) suggests that schools have explored various learning strategies during distance learning and "teachers and students and families have had more one-on-one conversations as they struggle to figure out the new normal." This situation to which many educators have adapted might actually help us be more open minded when it comes to opportunities for promoting effective communication. For example, some students often have difficulty looking directly into the eyes of another person and holding a meaningful conversation. Having students practice these skills through a virtual conference with just a few peers may be the option that works best for students who fear public speaking. Allowing students to give a presentation via laptop from the comfort of their home may put them at ease if they typically struggle with anxiety—and serve as the precursor to a successful in-person presentation they give before twenty-five classmates. Whatever the means, the goal of professional communication-skills attainment remains prominent.

With the influx of text messaging and various social media platforms, all of which require that people streamline the way they convey the written word, helping students master the art of communication offers a unique challenge. Teachers, media specialists, and counselors, for example, should share with students the proper uses of social media and other communication tools. Over time, students of all age groups should learn digital accountability and ethical usage of various social media platforms. In work environments, employees need to be able to choose appropriate uses for social media platforms, listen attentively, interpret nonverbal cues such as facial expressions, and interpret written procedural safeguards. Communication requirements call for employees to use these skills while they complete tasks such as brainstorming solutions to specific situations or providing concise information in written form.

Relay

Through discussion with stakeholders, including teachers and industry partners, students can learn and demonstrate, with the framework lessons and activities, how to make proper use of written, verbal, and nonverbal communication tools. The following activities are intended for teachers to use with their students and provide practical experience with communication skills. The first activity, paper folding, initially seems quite simple. However, because this process requires that students use their listening skills to interpret and act on verbal directions devoid of any visual assistance, it leaves room for students to come up with different results. The second activity is based on nonverbal communication within a group of people who work together to find a solution. This activity focuses on the reflection of processes, pattern comprehension, and effective nonverbal communication skills, which, when combined, allow all group members to successfully navigate a maze.

Our intention is not to create additional curricula for teachers but rather to integrate common terminology that connects needed skills to career readiness. The activities are designed to help students understand the concept of taking risks (as a leader), what constitutes an appropriate risk, and how responsibility relates to the role of communication in making plans for a project and relaying information to a team, department, or partner. Discussion further drives home the point to rationally think through problems and clearly communicate solutions.

PAPER FOLDING

This paper-folding activity, which we adapted from United States Institute of Peace (n.d.), allows students to understand subtle ways that different interpretations of verbal directions can alter an outcome. Students debrief with questions that give them the opportunity to respect diverse results and explanations. The activity goes on to show how one simple shift in decision making can lead one student down a path completely different from the paths of classmates. Note that if you find yourself in a virtual setting, this activity can readily be used through a Microsoft Teams or Zoom meeting, for example, and with any color or style of notebook paper.

Materials

Each student will need the following.

- 1 sheet of paper

Directions

To carry out the activity with students, follow these steps.

1. Give each student one sheet of notebook paper.

2. Offer the following verbal directions, pausing after each instruction to give the students time to comply. You should complete the activity along with the students using your own sheet of paper to further demonstrate the desired outcome. (If you are in an online classroom setting, simply

ask students to turn with their backs to the screen while they complete
the sequence of verbalized steps.)

   a. Pick up your sheet of paper, and hold it in front of you. Close your
      eyes, and listen carefully to the directions. You are not allowed to
      open your eyes during the process or ask any questions.

   b. Fold your sheet of paper in half.

   c. Now tear off the right corner.

   d. Fold the paper in half again, and tear off the left corner of the sheet.

   e. Turn the paper clockwise, and fold again.

   f. Now tear off the right corner of the folded paper.

3. After they've completed all instructions, ask students to open their eyes
   and open their papers. Hold your paper up for them to see, and then ask
   them to hold their papers up if they ended up with one, two, three, or
   more holes in their paper. It may or may not resemble a snowflake.

4. Ask participants to compare their sheets with one another. Ask why,
   if you did a good job of communicating and they did a good job of
   listening, all the sheets look different from one another in some way. You
   will probably get responses such as "You didn't let us ask any questions!"
   or "The way you gave us directions wasn't clear!"

Homestretch

The goal of this activity is to show students that people may interpret the same information in different ways. Discuss with the students this activity's goal. Then, ask them
what changes you could make to the activity's communication process if the goal were
to have everyone's snowflakes look exactly alike. What happened because the verbal
instructions did not include a visual representation? Students should understand that
they each processed the directions in their own way. They should also identify the
different ways each of them interprets information and realize that each interpreta-
tion leads to a varied outcome.

Encourage students to look around the room and identify the snowflakes that look
the most like theirs. You can then have students get into groups with the classmates
who have these similar outcomes and discuss the interpretations they made during
the instructions. Some students who do not typically work together may have pro-
duced similar designs; watch and listen to these small-group conversations. As the
instructor, pay close attention and consider separating similar thinkers from one
another as a way to provide a broader spectrum of interpretations in each group for
the next class project.

THE SILENT MAZE

In this activity, students practice listening and communicating nonverbally. They receive verbal instructions, and they work collectively to walk through a maze using only nonverbal cues to communicate with each other. At our career center, teachers participate alongside the students while our pathway coordinator directs the activity, whereas teachers in comprehensive classrooms conduct the activity and may not be able to join the action.

Ideally, adults should each have six to eight students assigned to their group. You will need to conduct the activity in a classroom with an open space at the front or rear, or in another place, such as a hallway or gymnasium.

Materials

To carry out this activity with students, gather the following items.

- A 6 × 8–foot tarp, per group of six to eight students
- Duct tape to create squares on the tarp
- A stopwatch, or cell phone with a stopwatch app
- The solution for how to walk through the maze (an example of which appears in figure 1.1)

					Finish
		X	X		X
		X		X	X
	X				
		X	X	X	
					X
	X	X		X	
	X		X		
	Start				

Figure 1.1: Maze solution.

Directions

To carry out the activity, follow these steps.

1. In preparation for the activity, lay out each tarp and use strips of duct tape to create a large grid of twelve-inch squares. For each tarp, on paper plot out a unique maze design, choosing an entrance square, an exit square on the opposite side, and a pathway in between.

2. Lay out the tarp—your maze—on the floor, taping down the corners to help keep it in place and prevent students from slipping. Make sure there is plenty of extra space around the perimeter of the tarp. Each student in the group will be expected to walk through the maze design while you monitor the completion of the task.

3. Stand near the exit that is shown for the maze. Let the students know that they have a job to do as a team, and direct them to the entrance side of the tarp. Explain that they must get from one side of the maze to the other side. Indicate that you know the way through because you are the maze wizard. Make sure that you have the maze's solution (figure 1.1, page 15) in hand and that students cannot see it.

4. Inform the students of the following rules.

   a. The team will have twenty minutes to complete the task.

   b. The team members can use three of those minutes to strategize if they want, but once the first team member steps on the maze, remaining members can no longer communicate verbally.

   c. Only one person can be on the maze at a time; other team members may point to, but not touch, the maze without penalty. For example, team members may nod, shake their heads, and suggest a possible next step by gesturing toward a space on the tarp.

   d. Participants cannot leave "bread crumbs"—scrap paper to help them remember the first few steps while they proceed to new steps—or write down clues to their path.

   e. Everyone must move through the maze consecutively. Once a participant makes it to a point and takes a wrong step, the participant must exit the maze, go to the end of the line, and allow the next person to begin from the first correctly identified space.

   f. Students may walk around the outside perimeter of the maze as the team members take turns.

    g. Feel free to make slight adjustments as needed. For example, students in wheelchairs may use a dowel rod or a yardstick to indicate their chosen points in the maze as they roll across the maze without penalty.

5. Inform the students of the following penalties.

    a. The team loses a minute of time if more than one person steps on or touches the maze at the same time.

    b. The team loses a minute of time if someone speaks after the first participant has stepped on the maze.

6. Allow the team to ask you questions to clarify instructions, which should take just a few minutes; however, if the team members start strategizing with one another, tell them that their time has started, and start the clock on your stopwatch.

7. Each time a wrong step is made, you, as the maze wizard, should shake your head, indicating that the step is wrong. When a student steps correctly, nod. Students may insist that when they are just "testing a box," it doesn't count as a full step. Remind them that once any part of their foot touches the tarp, that is a step, and if it is incorrect, they must return to the back of the line. The issue of integrity therefore becomes significant in this activity.

8. The activity is complete when each team member has successfully entered and exited the maze.

Homestretch

Once all teams have completed the maze activity, initiate a debriefing in which students share out about the process and discuss the difficulty of not being able to communicate verbally during most of the activity. Prompt students to talk through the decisions they made to ensure all team members successfully made it through the maze. (Amazingly, we used this activity with a group of sixty-eight students and eight adults, who all made it through without talking. There were cheers at the end, we will admit.)

Connecting this activity to real-world situations will further illustrate for students why they need to learn communication skills. For example, during the activity debrief at Hoosier Hills Career Center, a fire science instructor asked students to draw exactly how they went from one end of the maze to the other. As a group, the students went back to the maze to make sure they had the correct steps outlined. The fire science instructor then described search-and-rescue procedures and showed how this activity is precisely the same thing. He explained that once firefighters locate a surviving person in a burning building, they must secure the person and safely withdraw from the building in the exact way they came into it. Once outside, they draw and describe the pathway for the next crew member who enters to continue with the procedure. This crew is able to move carefully and more quickly to the last area in which a survivor was located and continue the methodical searching, moving along the perimeter of the building and often communicating with one another through hand gestures or tugs on the hose that serves as a guideline. If they do not give clear instructions to one another, it hampers the rescue and puts people in harm's way. This activity and apt analogy clearly show students that listening and nonverbal communication skills are vital in real-life scenarios—in the classroom, in the workplace, or elsewhere. These real-world connections make all the difference in students' learning.

Comprehensive classroom instructors or group leaders could use this activity to begin instruction on the topic of logical sequential actions and the result of correctly completing each action. As an example, you could connect this activity to mathematical processes or the scientific method to help students in groups understand their individual and collective roles in successful outcomes.

Conclusion

Effective communication is truly an art that a person must develop over time. Communication—verbal, nonverbal, and written—is a key skill necessary for success in the classroom and the workplace. Simple communication activities, like those in this chapter, can demonstrate to students that communication is a two-way process, involving sending and receiving information in various formats. This chapter targets ways teachers can connect these communication skills to practical applications, which translate to helping students meet industry needs. Communication is a foundational component of employability-skills training that demands intentional preparation and use with students. Watching as your students participate in communication is an amazing process.

CHAPTER 2

Teamwork and Collaboration

Teamwork and *collaboration*—these words are often used interchangeably to describe an essential component of workplace success. Teamwork may sound more familiar, as we often connect it to athletics. For example, on a basketball team, the point guard, forward, and center must fulfill their different roles, or carry out different tasks, working toward a common goal—positioning someone on their team to score points. But collaboration involves a group of people who share responsibility and think, plan, and work together, striving toward an agreed-upon solution. These competencies resonate with employers, and according to the Conference Board of Canada (n.d.) and the U.S. Department of Education's Office of Career, Technical, and Adult Education (2015), they are imperative for the workforce. Why is this the case? The answer is simple—teamwork and collaboration help promote sales, growth, productivity, and innovative ideas to stay ahead of competitors. These skills also provide employees with the ability to learn from their colleagues and find importance in others' ideas. These same skills prove to be ones that teachers work toward when they place into working groups students with varied learning styles and personal characteristics and give them the time and space to solve a problem or discuss a topic. To accomplish company success, employers want employees who work well with others and are locked in on the company vision. They need employees to have team goals clearly in mind. A collaborative approach makes group members feel comfortable bringing divergent ideas to the table and allows group members opportunities to persuade, convince, and negotiate agreements. A true collaboration or team blends the best of all and develops workable solutions, which is what we focus on in this chapter. Let's explore the rationale behind promoting teamwork and collaboration among students, the research that illustrates this skill set's relevance in the workforce, and activities that will help students gain proficiency with this skill set.

Rationale

An all-hands-on-deck team approach allows team members to gather information quickly. A truly collaborative team can do comprehensive analyses of ideas, make creative decisions, and often produce more prudent, and more profitable, results. Sometimes, a strong team can receive a poor plan yet craft it into a workable solution. However, not all teams are effective. Fragmented, uncooperative teams can take an inordinate amount of time reaching decisions, have frequent personality clashes, and negatively affect production.

In the classroom, you have the ability to strengthen personality traits that will lead students to become successful team members. Teachers have often paired students of differing abilities together to help bridge understanding among peers about how each person processes information. Educators all have tricks for partnering students, so we offer this suggestion from our classroom experiences. When focusing on employability-skills instruction, we have initial discussions about the types of careers that students gravitate toward. We use that information to group students with divergent interests—for example, placing in a group students who lean toward construction and those who wish to pursue culinary arts. They then work toward a common objective and devise a plan, carry out that plan, and, hopefully, meet the objective. As a way to initiate classroom dialogue on teamwork and collaboration, we use figure 2.1 as a handout and ask students to first reflect on the traits and their meanings. We then discuss the traits and share how they relate to working in a classroom or in the workplace.

Students' self-assessments often reveal that they have an unrealistic or biased view of themselves, rating their personal qualities as being either higher or lower than in reality or in other students' views. For this reason, consider the self-assessment a vocabulary-building assignment, and use the terms to compliment groups or students when they demonstrate the traits.

Now, how do you integrate and encourage these traits in your classroom? First, you must distinguish between *teamwork* and *groupwork*. We know that teamwork involves individuals fulfilling their unique roles as part of a shared goal. While groupwork may sound similar, it typically does not produce the same results. Can you recall classroom moments in which you mentioned working in groups only to face moans, eye rolls, and grimaces from many students, with perhaps a few students responding enthusiastically and wanting to help determine who should be in which group? Often, groupwork involves just one member, who cares deeply about the group's grade, doing most of the work while the others take a backseat on the project. Even when group members divide project tasks, someone may not follow through, and another person will need to pick up the slack because of the shared grade. Sometimes, a dominant personality

What personal strengths do you bring to a team? Rate your level of confidence for each trait by placing a check mark in the appropriate column.

Trait	What It Means	Not So Confident	Sort of Confident	Really Confident
Reliable	You can be counted on to get the job done.			
Effective Communicator	You express your thoughts and ideas clearly and directly, with respect for others.			
Active Listener	You listen to and respect different points of view. Others can offer you constructive feedback, and you don't get upset or defensive.			
Participates	You are prepared and get involved in team activities. You are a regular contributor.			
Shares Openly and Willingly	You are willing to share information, experience, and knowledge with the group.			
Cooperative	You work with other team members to accomplish the job, no matter what.			
Flexible	You adapt easily when the team changes direction or you're asked to try something new.			
Committed	You are responsible and dedicated. You always give your best effort.			
Problem Solver	You focus on solutions. You offer constructive criticism and are open to others' ideas.			
Respectful	You treat other team members with courtesy and consideration all the time.			
Tally your scores from the rightmost columns.				
Now consider your confidence levels and complete the following sentences. I am proudest of my ability to: I want to improve my ability to:				

Source: Adapted from U.S. Department of Labor, 2013.

Figure 2.1: Teamwork and collaboration skills inventory.

*Visit **go.SolutionTree.com/21stcenturyskills** for a free reproducible version of this figure.*

takes charge of the group and doesn't care to listen to what the others have to say. As a teacher, you should try to prevent such dynamics by organizing the teams yourself and giving specific tasks to each member.

It is important for students to work, and work well, with others in their classes. As you integrate the skill of teamwork into your lesson plans, you can teach appreciation of diversity and show students how a group of people can work toward a common goal through cooperation, collaboration, and expansion of ideas. Regularly putting your students into *different* teams is valuable in achieving this. You, as the classroom instructor, can offer a variety of learning situations to allow all students the opportunity to have success and to feel valued by their peers. Having activities that support your curriculum while addressing a variety of talent will help all students learn they bring value to a group, your class, and the workforce. We suggest that you build teamwork through striving for 100 percent student engagement in team projects—no grade, no right answer, just engagement. Grades have created a hierarchy in the traditional classroom. If you are serious about building collaboration in your classroom, eliminating the grade component will give you improved results, and according to the Center for Teaching Innovation (n.d.) at Cornell University, the use of self-assessment and peer assessment through such collaborative exercises will provide "preparation for real life social and employment situations."

Research

According to the National Association of Colleges and Employers (2019), teamwork and collaboration ranks second among essential career-readiness competencies on its *Job Outlook 2019* survey, falling behind only critical thinking and problem solving. The National Network of Business and Industry Associations' (2014) category of people skills acknowledges teamwork, communication, and respect as essential employability skills. Both organizations provide us with data on the importance of teamwork in the workplace.

In the mid-1960s, educational psychologist Bruce Tuckman branded four stages of team building, adding a fifth and final stage in the 1970s: (1) forming, (2) storming, (3) norming, (4) performing, and (5) adjourning. The following list describes what often happens when teams form, face challenges, and make progress toward solutions during these five stages (Mind Tools, n.d.b).

1. Forming
   - Team members get to know each other.
   - Most team members are usually positive and polite.
   - Team members may have some anxiety about their roles and the team's performance.

2. Storming

    - Frustration and conflicts occur.
    - Disagreements on the direction of the team arise.
    - Boundaries are pushed.
    - Team members need to pick their battles carefully.

3. Norming

    - Team members resolve issues and problems.
    - The team develops acceptance and respect.
    - Team members appreciate their differences.
    - Team members act as a team and focus on their mission.

4. Performing

    - The team has good communication.
    - Team members are confident, with a can-do attitude.
    - The team gets the job done.

5. Adjourning

    - The team dissolves because its project or season is over.
    - Individual team members move to different tasks.

As an educator, you must make it a goal to help students learn to move more efficiently through the stages of team building by understanding the factors that come into play. Educators need to accept that, initially, there may be barriers to working as a team, and they need to assist students in overcoming those barriers by setting clear expectations, providing instruction on preparedness, ensuring students' focus and engagement, and designing meaningful, relevant lessons. Management-training expert Carol Wilson (2010) offers further insight on Tuckman's stages, noting that because the global state of business is constantly in flux, tackling the stages is essential for stability and collaborative membership in the workforce. She adds, too, that people must focus on the foundational skills of coming together, setting boundaries, and achieving acceptance in order to open up new possibilities and solutions (Wilson, 2010). Such business strategies parallel those that educators seek to introduce into the classroom. Is this always easy? No. But as students develop more teamwork and collaboration skills, the classroom becomes a safer place and gives students a sense of belonging, in addition to equipping them with the means to be successful in the business world.

Relay

The development of skills comes with practice. If you want students to become proficient in collaborating and working together in groups, then you must structure activities to lead to the desired outcome. In this section, we include four activities for you to use that will allow students to collaborate in nonthreatening situations to develop these employability skills. The Ping-Pong ball container, boat-building, and bridge-building activities require students to work together, strategize, and use materials to construct objects that will allow them to meet a singular objective (for example, catching a ball or withstanding weight), while the quote activity allows for group collaboration and discussion but will appeal to learners who prefer to work with words.

The key is to use the activities with intentionality so students identify and develop each skill. Encourage students by acknowledging the positive traits of collaboration and teamwork they demonstrate in their teams. Do you see cooperation and respect for others' ideas, and are all members involved? If so, recognize those traits in students by offering verbal and written encouragement for being able to address the issues without your having to step in. Reinforce the expectation that students will develop good habits by practicing collaborative learning across the curriculum.

PING-PONG BALL CONTAINER

In this activity, students work in small teams to make a container that they can use to catch and hold a Ping-Pong ball when a team member drops the ball from eye level. The challenge of this activity is that each team receives only twelve straws and eighteen inches of masking tape for building the container. This activity demonstrates the basis of teamwork, in that each student will in some way be involved in the creation of the container, whether he or she provides verbal support or hands-on work. All will be engaged in the process in some manner, whether collaborating on the build or involved with the ball drop.

Materials

Each team of students will need the following.

- 12 plastic drinking straws
- 18 inches of masking tape
- Ping-Pong ball

Directions

To carry out the activity with students, follow these steps.

1. Divide the class into teams (with three to four students per team), and distribute the materials to each team.

2. Give teams ten minutes to use their materials to construct a container that will catch a Ping-Pong ball if the container is on the floor and the ball is dropped from eye level.

3. When the ten minutes is over, have each team select a member to be the ball dropper, who will stand over or next to the container and hold the ball at eye level.

4. Have the ball dropper place the container on the floor. Each ball dropper may have another member of the team act as an assistant, or crane operator. The crane operator's job is to move the ball dropper's hand for optimal placement.

5. Give each team three attempts to drop the ball into the container that they've placed on the floor. The container should remain in one place, and the ball dropper and crane operator position themselves around that location. Team members may talk among themselves and strategize. Any team that gets the ball to go in and stay in the container receives a point, and the team with the most points by the end of the three attempts wins the challenge.

After all teams have finished, allow students five minutes for reflection. Then invite them to report out by first providing their general comments and observations and then answering the following questions.

- How did you decide to construct your container?

- What was your plan?

- Did a leader emerge?

- Did everyone participate and have a voice?

- What would you do differently if given the challenge again?

- How does this activity relate to teamwork?

Each time that you do this activity, you will find teams using different strategies. Some will have the shortest person drop the ball, some will choose the most athletic person, and others will simply give the OK to the first person who volunteers to drop the ball. You will see different containers—square ones, cylindrical ones, woven ones, ones that are taped at the bottom to keep the ball from rolling out, and so on. There are no right or no wrong answers, only different approaches to the same problem. Activities like this teach students to accept failure but at the same time look for opportunities. Students may fail to keep their ball in the container, but they can look at the designs of the teams who were more or less successful and discuss what could have been done differently. Rarely does a team succeed at all three attempts, but if one does, that team could demonstrate the technique it used or even lead the other teams in better construction methods.

Homestretch

When you are focusing on teamwork, you are also enhancing other employability skills such as communication and problem solving. For instance, asking students to report out and letting them share the experience with you, and with one another, helps them strengthen communication skills without worrying about having the wrong answer. In this activity, you are not grading students on their designs or on the number of times the ball stays inside the container. Rather, students reflect on the skills they used and the ways they worked within the team. Being able to process and work through an activity without the fear of getting a poor assignment grade allows students to accept flawed designs and imagine improvements. Also, you can have students engage in problem solving by asking them what they might have done differently if they'd had more straws or more tape.

You could adapt this collaborative activity in numerous ways simply by having students build something else from a different set of materials; for example, you could have them build a tower from marshmallows and spaghetti or from note cards. Challenge yourself to tailor this team activity to your specific subject matter. If you are teaching about aqueducts in ancient Rome, for instance, you could have students create a series of paper tubes that carry the Ping-Pong ball to a container.

QUOTES ON WORKING TOGETHER

Teaching strategies need to support different student learning styles. This activity focuses on the verbal-linguistic learner, emphasizing reading, analysis of content, and the use of persuasion to express opinion. As it uses quotes as a vehicle for discussion, this teamwork and collaboration activity is well suited for English, social studies, business, and career classes. However, you could select teamwork quotes that support other disciplines, such as using quotes from coaches and athletes in a physical education class or quotes from inventors in a science class. For this activity, we've included three quotes as examples, but we recommend having between three and ten quotes as options to discuss, depending on your class size and the amount of time you're able to allot for the activity.

Materials

In order to carry out this activity with students, please gather the following.

- Quotes for students to review, such as these:
  - "Coming together is a beginning, staying together is progress, working together is success."—Henry Ford (Lagae, 2017)

+ "Talent wins games, but teamwork and intelligence wins championships."—Michael Jordan (Rogacka, 2020)

+ "Finding good players is easy. Getting them to play as a team is another story."—Casey Stengel (Rogacka, 2020)

Directions

To carry out the activity with students, follow these steps.

1. Pass out a sheet of paper with numerous quotes listed. Tell students to each select the quote they most relate to.

2. Have students get into groups of three or four, and ask that students each share their selection and reason for the selection with the group. Ask students to consider and discuss with one another which quote might best represent the group and why.

3. After small-group discussion, bring everyone back to the whole group, and have groups report out.

Homestretch

You can take this activity one step further and incorporate mathematics by tallying up students' choices and creating a graph or percentages. And whatever the content area into which you've embedded the activity, you can approach each quote in a variety of ways. Some students will gravitate to a quote based on the speaker or the speaker's profession, and others will focus on the sentiment of the message and relate to it directly. Regardless of students' choices, their reflection will spark interesting discussions as they work together and share with one another.

BUILDING A BOAT

You can have teams of students create boats that float using common school and household supplies. The objective of this activity is for students to see how much weight the boats that they build can withstand before they sink or collapse. All team members will collaborate on the design, weighing in and making joint decisions on the placement of straws and tape, how to utilize the foil, and so forth.

Materials

Each team of students will need the following.

• A 3 × 5–inch note card

• Unlimited masking tape

• 3 plastic drinking straws

- A 1 × 1–foot piece of aluminum foil
- A set of small objects to use as weights, such as pennies
- A large bowl of water or access to a sink

Directions

To carry out the activity with students, follow these steps.

1. Post the following directions for students on a whiteboard or flip chart.

   a. Requirements: Your boat must float and have a sail.

   b. 5 minutes: Collaborate and sketch.

   c. Get teacher approval of your sketch.

   d. 25 minutes: Build your boat.

   e. Present your design to the class.

   f. Test your boat's float and weight capacity.

2. Divide students into teams of three or four.

3. Inform students that the challenge for each team is to design and build a boat that will float. The goal is to build a boat that can float the longest while supporting the greatest amount of weight. The boat must include a sail.

4. Before distributing the materials, give the teams five minutes to collaborate, discuss, and sketch a boat design.

5. After five minutes of design time, have each team show its completed sketch to you in order to receive the materials.

6. Allow teams twenty-five minutes to build their boats.

7. When time is up, tell students that they must stop building and step away from their boats. One by one, teams should then present their boats to the class and explain why they chose their designs.

8. Finally, test the boats in water to see which one can support the heaviest weight for the longest amount of time. Students should place the boats in the water, and you should add the pennies or other weights to each boat until it no longer floats.

Homestretch

Have teams share out their processes for designing their boats. The team members whose boat held the most weight should elaborate on the specific details of their design. Ask questions about the design and the weights: Would the boat hold up better if the pennies were placed on top of each other in the craft or if the pennies were evenly distributed across the surface of the boat? What did the teams do to ensure their boats would not take on water? An open discussion about the processes and work done collectively is a great way to offer connections to a work environment.

BUILDING A BRIDGE

Similar to that of the preceding activity, the challenge here is to design and, using common supplies, build a foot-long bridge that will support the greatest amount of weight. You could use the activity in a middle school Project Lead the Way Gateway program or in a high school's introductory class on the principles of engineering. STEM groups may also be interested in this activity for a during-school or after-school project.

Materials

Each team of students will need the following.

- A 1 × 1–foot square of poster board
- 4 feet of masking tape
- 5 pipe cleaners
- 5 plastic drinking straws
- 1 pair of scissors (may not actually be used as a part of the finished design)

Directions

To carry out the activity with students, follow these steps.

1. Post the following directions for students on a whiteboard or flip chart.

    a. 5 minutes: Collaborate and sketch.

    b. Get teacher approval of your sketch.

    c. 30 minutes: Build your bridge.

    d. Present your design to the class.

    e. Test your bridge's weight capacity.

2. Divide students into teams of three or four.

3. Explain that the teams' task is to create a bridge that spans one foot and the goal is for their bridge to support the greatest amount of weight among all the designs.

4. Before distributing the materials, give the teams five minutes to collaborate, discuss, and sketch a bridge design.

5. After five minutes of design time, have each team show its completed sketch to you in order to receive the materials.

6. Allow teams thirty minutes to build their bridges.

7. When time is up, tell students that they must stop building and step away from their bridges. One by one, teams should then present their bridges to the class and explain why they chose their designs.

8. Finally, place the weights on each bridge until it is no longer able to maintain the weight and collapses.

Homestretch

Have students reflect on the activity and share what their teams did well and how their teammates could have worked together better. Did everyone participate? Did a leader emerge? To increase the fun factor of the bridge design, small toy cars would be a welcome weight addition for any age group.

Conclusion

As you use teamwork and collaboration activities in the classroom, keep in mind their primary purpose of helping your students practice and develop personal traits that will benefit them throughout their lives. Being able to work well with others is valuable in the classroom, in family life, and in the workplace. With your guidance, students will strengthen their employability skills through intentional practice.

CHAPTER 3

Critical Thinking and Problem Solving

“What do you think about . . . ?” and “What if . . . ?” form the basis of many questions educators pose to students in the classroom. But are students' answers superficial, or are they indicative of analytical thought? Do students base their responses on conclusions they've drawn from facts and logic or on anecdotal evidence and personal opinions? To address complex questions and real-world problems, students need the skills that top the National Association of Colleges and Employers' (2019) list of career competencies that employers value most: critical thinking and problem solving.

Can something like *critical thinking* be easily defined? Not quite. Throughout the educational realm, teachers, theorists, and philosophers have inserted their personal opinions when summarizing its meaning. Some describe critical thinking as a process, and others as the ability to engage in reflective and independent thinking. Problem solving and decision making may be included as part of critical thinking, or they may stand alone, depending on the education or industry resource one consults. For the purpose of this book, we will put problem solving and decision making in the same skill set as critical thinking, and we'll support this grouping with an activity in the Relay section of this chapter (page 34).

From critical thinking to problem solving, students must be equipped to identify an issue, brainstorm ideas, consider solutions and choose the most viable one, carry out a plan, and evaluate the results. Let's look more closely at the practical applications of this skill set in the workplace, the research that supports its inclusion in the employability-skills framework, and how teachers can encourage this skill set and help students develop it in the classroom setting.

Rationale

Whether their role involves products, services, or innovations, critical-thinking skills enable employees to approach their tasks thoughtfully and creatively, deftly solve work-related problems, and make sound decisions. When their staff are critical thinkers, companies can be forward thinking, anticipating customers' or clients' needs often before even those stakeholders consciously realize their needs.

When you look at accomplishments throughout history, you see how inspired thinking has indeed created the lives people lead in the 21st century. Who could have imagined that the telephone Alexander Graham Bell invented would be the forerunner of the smartphones people carry around today (Biography, 2019)? What about Garrett Morgan's invention of the three-light traffic signal, the direct result of his having witnessed an accident at an unsafe intersection? Who could have imagined that Morgan would use his mechanical-engineering skills to create a safer traffic light and sell the rights to that process to General Electric for further innovation (Biography, 2020)? During the Industrial Revolution, Cyrus McCormick's invention of the grain reaper did not readily catch on in the farming world until he started marketing the equipment with an installment payment plan—a novel idea in the marketplace that continues to be a common practice (Bellis, 2019).

The list of innovative ideas goes on and on, of course, including the internet, Apple, Google, Airbnb, and even bottled water. Critical thinking and creative thinking have transformed the business world, thereby influencing our daily lives and educational requirements.

Research

While we may notice, for example, an increase in organizations like C21 Canada (n.d.), a not-for-profit organization that helps to "[infuse] 21st century skills . . . into content and instructional and assessment practices," the big push in North American education to develop thinking skills is not new. At the beginning of the 20th century, psychologist John Dewey (1933) coined the term *reflective thinking* in his philosophy of education. *Reflective thinking* refers to the process that occurs when a student faces a real-world problem that requires observation and information gathering to come up with possible solutions. Once the student weighs the possible solutions, he or she takes action, testing the possibilities for a successful outcome (Dewey, 1933). Dewey believed the measure of students' educative growth is the quality of their mental processes, not just their ability to produce correct answers. In his later work, Dewey emphasized the importance of developing fundamental educational value in the daily routine of teaching, including the use of reflection, imagination, creativity, inquiry, communication, and judgment (Simpson & Stacks, 2010). In 2013, the

Partnership for 21st Century Learning acknowledged essential learning skills for the future that include the four Cs: (1) critical thinking, (2) communication, (3) collaboration, and (4) creativity (Battelle for Kids, n.d.). Decades apart, research points to the importance of teaching critical thinking.

In 1941, psychologist Edward Glaser stated that the ability to think critically has three components:

> (1) an attitude of being disposed to consider in a thoughtful way the problems and subjects that come within the range of one's experiences, (2) knowledge of the methods of logical inquiry and reasoning, and (3) some skill in applying those methods. (Foundation for Critical Thinking, n.d.)

In the 1960s, Robert Ennis (2011) presented a basis of twelve abilities of critical thinking; these became the foundation of his later work to define *critical thinking* as "reasonable and reflective thinking focused on deciding what to believe or do." Throughout the 1970s and 1980s, an emphasis on reasoning and logic for the college student came to the forefront. Even so, industry felt that the U.S. education system was falling short of preparing students for the workforce. Employers needed employees who had the ability to learn and contribute as members of a team. Therefore, in 1991, the Secretary's Commission on Achieving Necessary Skills (SCANS) was appointed to determine the preparation that U.S. students require to meet world-class workplace standards. SCANS found that all high school students need five broad competencies—(1) resources, (2) interpersonal skills, (3) information, (4) systems, and (5) technology—and a three-part foundation of basic skills, thinking skills, and personal qualities (U.S. Department of Labor, 1991). The SCANS report defines those foundational *thinking skills* as "thinking creatively, making decisions, solving problems, seeing things in the mind's eye, knowing how to learn, and reasoning and integrity" (U.S. Department of Labor, 1991, p. vii).

In the 21st century, industry identifies the skill of critical thinking as one of the most important employee attributes. The U.S. Department of Labor's industry competency model identifies creative thinking, problem solving, and decision making as workplace competencies, and critical and analytical thinking as an academic competency. This indicates the importance of teaching these essential skills to better prepare students for the workplace (Competency Model Clearinghouse, n.d.).

Industry has developed critical-thinking models, including Six Sigma, the five whys, and the fishbone diagram, that assist employees in finding the root cause of an issue. Looking at these models can give educators insight into workplace strategies that they can use as references when teaching critical thinking.

With Six Sigma, six to fifteen team members work together and follow specific steps—define, measure, analyze, improve, and control—to create a process map and ultimately target a problem and improve the quality of operations. Though Six Sigma was originally created to eliminate waste and bring about a more effective production system, numerous companies that wish to evaluate and potentially overhaul their current processes and practices provide their staff with Six Sigma training. Employees earn belts based on their competencies and levels of proficiency, with white, yellow, green, black, and master black belts awarded (Purdue University, n.d.).

Employees also utilize the five whys strategy to find the underlying cause of a problem. In the case of this strategy, the employees with hands-on experience with the problematic situation become the experts, and after identifying the problem, they determine what is causing the problem by asking, "Why?" Answers must be factual and specific. The process continues, with the experts asking, "Why?" four or more times through a single lane, or multiple lanes, of inquiry. When the experts are no longer generating useful responses, the group decides on a countermeasure or process change (Mind Tools, n.d.a).

The cause-and-effect diagram, often referred to as the *fishbone diagram*, requires team members to consider the major categories of a problem's causes; these categories can include methods, machines and equipment, people and manpower, materials, measurement, and environment (American Society for Quality, n.d.). This strategy helps employees identify the factors behind a system failure—or why a process needs to be revised. Those with careers in manufacturing and health care might use the fishbone diagram to problem solve. Understanding of what is happening in industry can help educators set parameters to facilitate students' use of critical-thinking and problem-solving skills. Our colleagues in Australia have been focusing instruction on this precise skill area to assist potential employees with their ability to "recognize that identified problems can be surface indicators of deeper issues" and reinforce their capacity for "identifying a root cause" (Australian Government, 2020).

Research clearly outlines the need for skills such as critical thinking and problem solving as they pertain to personal, educational, and professional settings. The ability to process information, ask questions, analyze data, and ferret out the possibilities to make a sound, logical decision will help students build the personal and professional skills necessary for a successful transition to employment. Educators can provide the training, as well as the practical application of these key skills across the curriculum, from algebra to poetry to agriculture.

Relay

You as the teacher must show students that they need to use knowledge, facts, and data to come up with solutions and better assess the situation when presented with a problem. You can scaffold opportunities for the students to find alternative ways of viewing problems, work through problems, accept failures, and move forward again.

TRIANGLE TOOTHPICKS

The following triangle-toothpicks activity provides students with practice in creative thinking and problem solving, and it reinforces the idea that there can be multiple answers to a problem.

Materials

Each group of students will need the following.

- 6 toothpicks

Directions

To carry out the activity with students, follow these steps.

1. Divide the class into groups of three to four students.

2. Give each group six toothpicks.

3. Tell the groups their task is to arrange the toothpicks into four triangles. (Depending on the age and ability of the students, this task may take three to five minutes.)

There are several possible solutions, with no wrong answer and no *best* answer—so long as the design produces only four triangles. Probably the most common configuration is a square with an *X* inside; four toothpicks form the sides of the square, and two toothpicks run diagonally from corner to corner. After each group creates one design, challenge the students to rearrange the toothpicks and find other solutions. How many solutions can each group come up with? Do any of the groups make a 3-D design, with three toothpicks lying flat to form a triangle base and the remaining three toothpicks leaning against one another to create a pyramid?

Homestretch

The triangle-toothpicks activity allows students to explore answers to a problem in a nonthreatening way while participating as members of a group. You may debrief further by discussing with your students the importance of critical thinking, creativity, and innovation, particularly when resources are limited.

WHAT WOULD YOU DO?

In this activity, students work through problem-solving steps to determine a possible solution to a given problem.

Materials

Ensure each student has the following.

- 1 What Would You Do? worksheet (figure 3.1)
- 1 What's Your Problem? worksheet (figure 3.2, page 38)
- 1 pen or pencil

Directions

To carry out the activity with students, follow these steps.

1. Review the following basic problem-solving steps with students.

   a. Identify and define the problem.

   b. Brainstorm ideas for possible solutions; try to come up with at least three ideas that might work.

   c. Consider the potential pros and cons of each option.

   d. Choose what seems to be the best option.

   e. Carry out the plan.

   f. Evaluate whether the plan worked.

2. Have students individually complete the What Would You Do? worksheet (figure 3.1).

3. To enhance a personal connection to problem solving, have students complete the What's Your Problem? activity (see figure 3.2, page 38).

Homestretch

Companies want employees who can think on their feet, assess difficult situations, and weigh multiple solutions before ultimately tackling a problem. As an educator, you can adapt the What Would You Do? worksheet (figure 3.1) to include other scenarios for students' consideration, such as the issues of hunger in the community, weekend activities for youth, and technology training for employed adults.

DECISION MAKING

The decision-making process is a logical, sequential way to make a choice or solve a problem. According to UMass Dartmouth (n.d.), the seven-step process is as follows: (1) identify the decision you must make, (2) collect information, (3) determine the possible paths you may take, (4) evaluate the evidence, (5) choose among the paths, (6) carry out the decision, and (7) assess the outcome of your decision.

Directions: Some of the problems we encounter in life raise serious ethical questions, forcing us to consider our value systems in making important decisions. This makes for a thoughtful and time-consuming process as we weigh pros and cons of issues that may be controversial or have no clear-cut answers. Carefully consider the following scenario, and then write out your process for the solution you develop.

You're riding the bus on the way to school one morning, and once the bus stops and you prepare to exit, you see a twenty-dollar bill on the floor. You bend down to pick it up and place it in your pocket. In your first-period class, you sit next to a good friend, whom you tell about your lucky find. Your friend suggests that you report the lost money to the office and have staff check with students from the bus to see whether the owner of the money can be found.

1. Identify the problem.

   _____

   _____

   _____

2. Determine the options.

   a. _____

   b. _____

   c. _____

3. Evaluate the options.

   a. _____

   b. _____

   c. _____

4. Choose the best option.

   _____

   _____

   _____

5. Make a plan.

   _____

   _____

   _____

6. Carry out the plan.

7. Evaluate the results.

   _____

   _____

   _____

Figure 3.1: What Would You Do? worksheet.

*Visit **go.SolutionTree.com/21stcenturyskills** for a free reproducible version of this figure.*

Name: _____ Date: _____ Period: _____

What's Your Problem?

Directions: Identify a problem that a high school student may need to solve. Use this flowchart to help map out its possible solutions. Select at least three solutions that might help solve the problem. Evaluate each solution for its pros (good things) and cons (bad things) if it were to be implemented. Then select the solution that you feel is best.

Problem:

WHAT'S YOUR PROBLEM?

↓

Possible Solution 1:

Pros:

Cons:

↓

Possible Solution 2:

Pros:

Cons:

↓

Possible Solution 3:

Pros:

Cons:

Which solution would you choose? Why?

Source: © 2016 by Davis & McBride Educational Consultants, LLC. Used with permission. Adapted by Londa Hight, Owen Valley High School, Spencer, Indiana.

Figure 3.2: What's Your Problem? worksheet.

*Visit **go.SolutionTree.com/21stcenturyskills** for a free reproducible version of this figure.*

When you present the decision-making process to students, thoroughly discuss each step so students understand the role it plays. Have students brainstorm a list of decisions they make on a daily or even weekly basis. Ideas might include what to eat, what to wear, when to go to bed, and what to do on the weekend. Then discuss with them when the decision-making process is helpful with regard to education and work. Example educational and professional choices include:

- Which occupation or career field to enter
- Which training to take or which education program to enter
- Which part-time job to work while in high school
- Whether to go directly to work or to go to college after high school
- Which high school courses to take
- Whether to change jobs

The following activity provides one means of conveying the importance of each step in the decision-making process.

Materials

Ensure each student has the following.

- 1 decision-making process note sheet (figure 3.3, page 40)
- 1 pen or pencil

Directions

To carry out the activity with students, follow these steps.

1. Tell students to imagine that they are high school seniors and they have quite a few tasks to complete by the end of next week, which include the following.

    - A scholarship essay that will take roughly forty minutes to write and is potentially worth one thousand dollars
    - A four-page English paper on the novel they just read that will take at least four hours to write and comprises 30 percent of the final grade
    - A community-service activity that will take three hours to complete but can be done whenever they choose
    - An extra task that their boss at their part-time job has assigned to them that will take one hour to complete

2. Ask students to ponder the question, "In which order will you decide to complete these tasks, and why?" Have them individually complete the decision-making process note sheet (figure 3.3), which requires them to use the decision-making process to make an informed decision.

Step 1: Identify the problem.	
Step 2: Determine the options.	
Step 3: Evaluate the options.	
Step 4: Choose the best option.	
Step 5: Make a plan.	
Step 6: Carry out the plan.	
Step 7: Evaluate the results.	

Figure 3.3: Decision-making process note sheet.

*Visit **go.SolutionTree.com/21stcenturyskills** for a free reproducible version of this figure.*

Homestretch

Have students discuss their priority list from the decision-making process note sheet. Determine which task most students cited as the number-one priority, and ask that the students give their reasoning for the choice. Were there similarities in their decision making? Follow up by having students consider what they learned about decision making and prioritization from this activity that they will likely need to apply in the workplace.

Conclusion

Teachers often get caught up in having the "right" answer. But in reality, of course, some decisions have right answers, and some can be addressed in a variety of ways. For example, take your daily lesson plans. Are your plans in the same format as those of all the teachers in your building or school corporation? And if they are in the same format because of your school's requirements, do they all contain the same details? Do all the faculty members have the same number of days planned ahead for the school year? And do all the teachers arrive and leave school at exactly the same time? You and your fellow teachers each problem solve to find out what works best for you while meeting the needs of your students and the requirements of your employers. Teachers throughout your building or school corporation have used their critical-thinking skills to reach different determinations about these topics in order to meet their and their students' specific needs. Likewise, they have evaluated situations, carried out plans, and then re-evaluated outcomes to determine what they need to change. This is an ongoing cycle of decision making reflected in both education and industry.

As an educator, your job, in part, is to help students develop essential thinking skills to best meet future employers' requirements and future positions' needs. In your teaching, strive to provide learning opportunities that enhance critical and innovative thinking. If your students practice decision making, learn there can be multiple solutions, and cultivate the ability to weigh consequences and outcomes, they'll be better prepared for their next steps. With the rapid growth of technology and automation, critical thinking is more relevant than ever before because of the constantly changing job market. Each day your students are in your classroom, and even after they leave, you are instrumental in ensuring they have the essential tools for current and future successes.

CHAPTER 4

Workplace Relationship Building

What are the characteristics of effective relationships? To what extent is trust expected or earned? Would you say that trust comes into play in workplace relationships as often as it does in personal relationships? Do respect and interpersonal skills come to mind when you think about your friends, family, and coworkers? How do people ensure equitable relationships in which all members feel comfortable speaking up—and feel that their voices are heard and valued? These are all questions that we'll answer in this chapter as we explore the qualities needed for positive, successful relationships, especially in the workplace. Effective workplace relationships may encompass teamwork and collaboration but build on and enrich these skills by adding the element of trust, particularly when it comes to participants' level of comfort sharing their ideas; team members must know that their colleagues view their ideas and proposed solutions as valid. This chapter addresses the importance of fostering positive relationships among a diverse workforce and the power of effective collaboration among various roles in an organization, and it supports a need to ensure progressive work settings. Treating colleagues with respect and assuring others of their importance and valuable contributions to a work environment keep effectiveness and efficiency as a central focus. Let's explore the rationale behind promoting relationship-building skills among students, the research that illustrates this skill set's relevance in the workforce, and activities that will help facilitate this skill development in students.

Rationale

Numerous business partners cite working well with others as a key quality among employees. In our original conversations with an advisory group from Hoosier Hills

Career Center, business leaders ranging from health care to construction, automotive industry to food services, shared that the top three things necessary for workplace success were being on time, passing a drug screen, and working well with others. It seems like it should be easy to meet this requirement, yet conflicts do happen in the workplace.

To help students understand the relationship skills that employers desire, we use social media messaging to break down the ways conflict can occur unintentionally. For example, social media can create distance between individuals, leaving some people feeling as though they can say anything they wish to anyone they please—whether what they say is hurtful or dishonest. And in the 21st century, students tend to make quick decisions as they relate to technology, hastily leaving comments on social media platforms that mirror the fleeting conversations they might have with their friends in person. Because of the hurried lifestyles they and many people lead, students leverage available resources to take these types of actions as they attempt to connect with one another. But students and adults sometimes forget that social media is easily tracked even if they'd like to think of it as personal and private. Even when students rethink and delete their questionable posts, their digital footprints remain, and employers can find the content if they know how to look deeply enough. Often, employers will turn to the internet to check their applicants' social media footprints to see what types of characteristics individuals show in global and unfiltered settings, and applicants' use of various social media outlets can be a factor in their getting a job offer. People who choose to make inappropriate statements on social media, or who post memes whose meanings they don't fully comprehend, can be eliminated from possible career positions. Additionally, employees are sometimes fired for posting comments regarding company happenings or specifics about their employers. For example, an in-the-know employee might think posting about an upcoming merger is harmless or might even be welcome news to friends in the community, but if the company has not publicly announced the merger, it could jeopardize the process.

Preparing for career success should cause students to think before they speak or post on social media. Once they make a comment, they cannot unmake that comment. It is critical for students to consider not just how they feel or think in the moment but how people will interpret their words and how those words can negatively impact themselves and others in the long term. Careless actions and comments preclude effective relationships; professional interpersonal connections, both face-to-face and via social media, are paramount for successful working relationships.

A real-world situation comes to mind—in which social media posts *positively* influenced one's initial impression to an employer. A former student recounted to us the time when, during her senior year in high school, she was nervous to attend an interview at a local motorcycle sales and repair business. We must note that this was a female student competing in a typically male-dominated career field, automotive collision repair, for employment with a company recognized internationally in the motorcycle arena. Her auto-collision teacher had arranged the interview for a Saturday morning and told her to make sure she brought her résumé. It was important that she present herself as confident in her talents and abilities while sharing her passion for the automotive industry and in particular custom motorcycles. As she walked into the store manager's office, she reached out and shook his hand and gave him her paperwork. After the initial greeting, he said, "Tell me about the seat cover you designed for this bike." She was stunned that he had printed off full-color images of various seat covers she had designed and sewn and then posted on social media. He laid them out on his desk as items to discuss during their interview in an attempt to show that he was interested in the work she was doing to create original designs for her clients. He had done his research to make sure not only that she was, on paper, serious about the industry but that her outside interests—in this case, custom creations for upscale-motorcycle enthusiasts—were consistent with the business's image and focus. While she was initially taken aback that the manager had looked at her Facebook and Instagram posts, she was pleased that he saw her as the artistic designer that she was and praised her unique creations. She had been involved in an unpaid internship with a terrific mentor upholsterer and was ready to get into the profession and be paid for her work. He shared that he was impressed not only with her talent and vision but with how she maintained a professional presence in person and on social media. This open conversation made it possible to establish an effective workplace relationship from the first meeting and afforded her the assurance that she was entering a workplace built on equitable opportunities. When the student went to class the following Monday, she shared with classmates the extent to which the manager had gone and how she was so glad that she had not embarrassed herself or regretfully posted anything negative online. She kept her posts focused on her upholstery work, and her dog, and left the more-personal information off social media. Powerful lesson for a high school student to share with her peers.

Research

Respectful behavior, understanding of diversity, and openness to others' opinions are foundational for successful collaboration and efficacy in a workspace. Valuing others' input and work is key to relationship building. These are not new concepts, as Harry Newton Clarke (1934), in *Career Planning and Building*, outlines the attitudes he designates as *horsepower* and *heartpower*. He writes that the two differ in focus, with horsepower encompassing the mechanical, or technical, components of business and heartpower representing the human-relations aspects of business. Clarke's (1934) data on industries at the beginning of the 20th century reveal that in conflicts that arose, 75 percent of the issues were in the area of heartpower rather than horsepower. And

Shelley Zalis (2017), senior contributor for *Forbes*, writes that diversity in particular leads to more creative teams and increases the company's bottom line. We must "be intentional about bringing diversity into meetings and work opportunities" and make sure people feel heard and have a sense of belonging—which increases work ethic, because colleagues then feel a sense of ownership of a company (Zalis, 2017). When people "embrace and respect individual strengths and create a collaborative and safe space," they prove that they value relationship building in the work environment (Zalis, 2017). Note that a true appreciation of diverse populations should move beyond a simple understanding of federal laws, which protect against discrimination in the workplace. Listening to and being receptive to ideas from all people within a group, rather than having only a single voice lead all decisions, helps enhance the possible solutions or outcomes.

In *A Framework for Understanding Poverty: A Cognitive Approach*, author and educator Ruby K. Payne (2019) discusses the importance of understanding various groups' mores as they relate to building effective relationships toward school-based achievement and workplace success. Think about the simple interactional elements that can serve as a key factor in getting a job offer. One such element is the impact of a first impression—or how a firm handshake and open body language might exhibit positive engagement. What might seem natural or expected in certain workplace situations might not be clearly understood across all groups of your students. For example, depending on her background or culture, a young woman might instinctively feel it's inappropriate to shake hands with a man who is conducting a meeting or an interview—and the man might interpret that as her not wanting to be a team member, simply because her behavior doesn't fit what he sees as standard practice. Likewise, a shy young man who responds briefly to questions and does not engage in small talk may be seen as standoffish or even rude. The variations in personality that students bring to the classroom follow them into the workplace and must be discussed to help adequately prepare students for the transition. Educators must consider these sometimes-puzzling driving forces from all students' perspectives. While it is important for teachers to discuss and demonstrate these and other basics of making a good first impression, they must keep in mind practical and equitable ways to introduce concepts surrounding these customs. Payne (2019) outlines group rules and provides a basis for understanding students' actions so that teachers can meet students where they are and assist them in getting what they want and where they want to be, rather than imposing their own desires onto the students. Initiating from this baseline allows you, as a practitioner, to work alongside your students on the journey to self-actualization and acceptance of individual goals and aspirations.

Secondary and postsecondary schools can create a more productive workforce through training on adaptability, professionalism, and interpersonal skills. These skills allow employees to move beyond superficial comments into trusting conversations; they serve as the foundational aspects of positive workplace interactions. Essential to an effective team of employees is their knowledge that equity goes beyond just attempting to make things available to all people, and creates ways to help overcome barriers that keep teams from moving forward.

Effective schools and businesses make all people feel integral to the problem-solving process and valued for their individual contributions to targeted outcomes. In "How to Build Effective Working Relationships," an article for the *Houston Chronicle*, writer Janice Tingum (2019) discusses the necessity of examining and taking a sincere interest in others' divergent perspectives if teammates are to build trust and really be respectful of one another. Whether in the classroom or a work environment, they all need to believe they are significant participants. Remaining consistent and dependable in all aspects of the workplace relationship is important. Think through a time when you felt someone didn't value your insights or suggestions, and reflect on the extent to which that affected you. Imagine that happening in a work setting. What type of employee might you become if you felt that you were not respected, listened to, and valued? According to writer Tori Fica (2019), in the business world, employee relationships that lack a sense of trust and importance lead to disengaged workers, which can be expressed through poor attendance or lack of attention to detail—which can then lead to poor-quality workmanship or defects, as well as accidents in the workplace.

Authors Alan S. Berson and Richard G. Stieglitz (2013) identify the four types of professional relationships that have their place in a successful business: (1) targeted relationships, (2) tentative relationships, (3) transactional relationships, and (4) trusted relationships. Berson and Stieglitz (2013) note that these relationships are all distinctive in their roles yet pivotal to business owners and those who work for the business. The trusted relationships take the longest to form and require the most work to sustain, but they result in huge impacts, both personal and professional (Berson & Stieglitz, 2013). One such impact is the ability of team members to coalesce around a shared objective, finding a solution through extensive conversations and the exchange of ideas. And diversity within the trusted group helps a business or team maintain balance in direction toward possible solutions, with input coming from varied perspectives. Nurturing strong relationships built on trust and transparency takes a great deal of time and effort, but Berson and Stieglitz (2013) remind us that individuals will be judged not only on their own merits but on the success of their teams and what they collectively are able to produce. Maintaining positive workplace relationships is an essential component of the employability-skills framework.

Relay

Teachers can connect students with the kinds of intentional interpersonal relationships they'll need in a work environment by offering them opportunities to work collaboratively in relaxed and engaging classroom activities. The skills necessary to connect with school peers mirror those required of work colleagues. Having an ability to share opinions openly and remain trustworthy and respectful during difficult discussions helps students establish positive and effective relationships. With the goal of coming up with a single answer to a given problem, teammates practice the valuable skills of flexibility, adaptability, and compromise while working together and working toward a positive outcome. Our framework stresses collaboration instead of competition in the workplace, with all students, or colleagues, striving for the same end goals while maintaining mutual respect for one another. These skills often start from different places depending on the group norms or rules of behavior ingrained in students, as Payne (2019) makes clear. Prior to initiating the activities, take the time to discuss these hidden rules to ensure that students don't take them for granted.

FLIP THE BLANKET

This activity requires participants to work collaboratively to turn a blanket or tarp over from side A to side B—while everyone stands on top of it. It stimulates lots of discussion at the end. The size of the blanket or tarp will determine the number of participants. There should be only about one-quarter of the blanket left as open space once all participants are standing on it. Typically, you will have five to seven participants per group, with all groups working on the task simultaneously.

Materials

For this activity, you'll need the following.

- A 4 × 6– or 5 × 5–foot blanket or tarp

Directions

To carry out the activity with students, follow these steps.

1. Lay the blanket (or tarp) flat. If you are inside the school building, it would be best to use a carpeted area rather than a tiled floor. If you can do this outside on a paved area or in a grass-covered location, that would also work. Just ensure that there is enough friction so that the blanket or tarp will not slip and cause a student to fall.

2. Have the group start out standing on the blanket.

3. Tell the group members that their task is to find a way to flip or turn the blanket over, from side A to side B. Keep in mind there is no time

limit imposed on this activity, though you may provide one if that suits your needs.

4. State that the group members may not step off the blanket at any time, and they may not use their hands during the activity. If someone violates one of these rules, the group will have to start over.

5. Once all groups complete the task, have the group members discuss the relationship skills they used to accomplish the task, sharing out one or two items per group as you take comments around the room or activity area.

Homestretch

Something as simple as flipping a blanket from one side to the other as a group may reveal who can lead, who can process, and who will follow until they are sure they have a better plan of action—and each of these roles is important for the group's success. Those who have participated in this activity maintain that *everyone* has to concentrate on the end results in order for the group to meet the objective, and reliance on others and trust in leadership and direction are a must.

MAKE IT THROUGH THE LAVA

This activity, which we adapted from a cooperative-games session we participated in at the Indiana State University (n.d.) Keystone Adventure Program, is about working in a supportive way to get your group from one rocky ledge to the other through a lava-filled gorge. Group members must discover their own means of staying connected with one another and making it across the terrain with what they have been provided.

Materials

For this activity, you'll need the following.

- Masking tape
- 30–35 paper plates

Directions

To carry out the activity with students, follow these steps.

1. Prepare to use a large portion of the room, or a hallway that you can section off, and use pieces of masking tape to mark a starting point and an ending point, with approximately fifteen feet between them. (Alternatively, if you choose to do this outdoors, you could use some other marker, such as a piece of rope.)

2. Divide the class into groups of five to six students, and give one paper plate to all but one member of each group.

3. Explain to students that, starting at one end of the masking tape, they must travel across the gorge by means of stepping-stones—the paper plates.

4. Give the students a few caveats: Group members must stay connected physically, such as by holding hands, and they cannot step in the lava, or off the paper plates. If a group member steps into the lava, the team will have to restart its travel across the gorge.

Some students may ask if they can tear the plates into two pieces; this is acceptable as long as group members stay connected while they cross. One possible solution might include students' using paper-plate halves for their feet and instructing the last (plateless) person to piggyback on the second-to-last participant.

Homestretch

It can take as little as fifteen minutes or as long as forty minutes for all teams to bridge the gorge. The key to this activity is class discussion about the methods groups used and the different ways that they may have tried, failed, tried again, failed again, and eventually found success. Groups often enjoy telling of their struggles and sharing what worked. Likewise, some students may enjoy discovering that their group came up with the most innovative or unique solution. Ultimately, the activity and subsequent discussion result in participants gaining a clearer understanding of the vital roles of communication, diverse ideas, and collective work, and they help to establish relationships and connections of trust and respect.

Conclusion

Effective relationships come in various forms and serve a variety of needs. If students put time and effort into building with others relationships that are characterized by trust, they will achieve personal and professional success. The diverse world in which they live offers a mountain of experience that they can learn from and grow within to become the best human beings possible.

Intentionally encouraging students to become effective in all their relationships offers educators the opportunity to teach across the curriculum and integrate employability skills necessary for students' successful transition as professionals—and as productive members of society. Incorporating these concepts into reflective writing exercises for the English or psychology classroom integrates ESSA's college- and career-readiness standards and state academic standards. Using the employability-skills activities precisely as written is certainly one option, but the goal here is to utilize these employability-skills components in previously established lessons rather than increase the number of modules. We would not be using the research in this chapter effectively if we ultimately failed to appreciate all that practitioners aim to teach students in a very limited amount of time. We simply offer vetted options from our boots-on-the-ground teaching colleagues who have successfully created cohesive standards and skills lessons that engage both them and their students. Ultimately, our high school–level colleagues have shared that students seem to respect them for making career skills part of the academic classroom.

As a way of walking our talk, we have focused our goals in this chapter on the development of personal and professional relationships through discussions of trust and, for example, the hidden rules of those with whom we work and collaborate. We want to help you answer student questions such as "How will we ever use this in the future?" and indeed help you rely on our framework. We hope that the relationship we have built up to this point in the text allows you to continue trusting our framework and to engage your students in such a way that it leads to authentic conversations.

On a more global note, people's futures as employees, parents, significant others, and friends are impacted by their relationship choices. Strive to help your students become effective builders of positive relationships across all arenas, which will assist them in contributing to their personal and professional lives in meaningful ways.

CHAPTER 5

Resource Management

One might ask, "Why include resource management in an employability-skills framework?" And a justified answer might be that in the workplace, managing time, money, materials, and personnel is valued. However, our answer goes beyond this simplified explanation. Our students have come to us facing numerous barriers—having experienced poverty, homelessness, domestic violence, neglect, substance abuse, foster care, and the juvenile justice system. We are sure you could add to the list of student barriers—so many different childhoods, so many different obstacles to overcome. As we are supporters of teaching the whole child, our goal is to eliminate as many barriers as possible so that our students can thrive. Using resource management—whether learning self-management strategies or reaching out to agencies for support—can assist students in dealing with the impact of adverse childhood experiences and future family dynamics. If we can help reduce the level of stress associated with a student's situation, the student will be able to focus on instruction. Beyond this, the World Economic Forum (2020b) reports that self-management—including active learning, resilience, and stress tolerance—is an emerging top skill that employers want. Such resource-management skills are beneficial to all students when it comes to both overcoming obstacles and plotting a course to adulthood.

Students need to learn that they possess the resources of knowledge, skills, and time. They also need to be introduced to community agencies and resources so that they develop civic engagement and know where to go for help if life takes a negative turn. Knowing individual and community resources can impact their quality of life—for today and tomorrow. Let's take an even closer look at the rationale behind fostering resource management, the research that illustrates this skill's relevance in the workforce, and specific activities that will help facilitate this skill development in students.

Rationale

Often, educators have to deal with emergency situations by connecting students to services as an intervention tool. There is nothing wrong with this type of assistance; in fact, the help offers tremendous support for students in need of services. For example, in situations in which students do not have sufficient food at home or they lack winter coats, administration and the guidance department are the first line of defense and connect students and their families to the agencies that will best meet their needs. But within the employability-skills framework, our mission is twofold: (1) to teach students about how to manage individual resources of knowledge, skills, and time and then (2) to introduce students to the types of broader resources available in their own communities, which they can explore through service-learning opportunities.

According to the Annie E. Casey Foundation's Kids Count Data Center (2019), which analyzed 2018 data from the U.S. Census Bureau, 18 percent of youth under the age of eighteen live in poverty, which, for a family of two adults and two children, translates to an annual income below $25,465. Think about that statistic for a moment—a family of four living on less than $26,000 a year and working to afford shelter; food; clothing; and medical, dental, and vision care. Educators need to consider the home lives of the students they serve. According to the U.S. Department of Health and Human Services' Office of Population Affairs (2019), those who grow up in poverty are more likely to have social, emotional, and behavioral problems and experience suppressed cognitive development and academic achievement.

Such data offer a glimpse into the situation but may seem somewhat clinical. Personally, you can get a rough sense of the poverty level among students in your school by reviewing the free- and reduced-lunch statistics. From our personal observations as educators, elementary school free- and reduced-lunch data are usually more reliable because secondary school students are less likely to submit forms to receive free or reduced lunch, with reasons ranging from they don't want others to know about their situations to they pay their own way with income from part-time jobs. If you are in a secondary school setting, know that some of your students may be working between thirty-two and forty hours a week while being full-time students. That places a huge demand on high school students and may lead to their being late to school, sleeping during class time, or having attendance issues or negative attitudes. As educators, we find that students often work late into the evening to contribute to their family's income and household items, paying for clothes, a car, gas, car insurance, and all things school related, especially senior-year expenses. These financial responsibilities often impact academic performance and attitude toward school.

Introducing students to the concept of how to capitalize on personal assets, such as being reliable and punctual, contributing effectively as team members, and holding themselves accountable for results, will help all students set themselves apart in the workplace and better navigate current and future family dynamics.

Research

In its employability-skills framework, the U.S. Department of Education's Office of Career, Technical, and Adult Education (2015) lists resource management—that is, managing time, money, materials, and personnel—as a primary component of essential workplace skills. Everyone has 24 hours, 1,440 minutes, or 86,400 seconds each day, and it's up to each person to maximize that time to achieve short- and long-term goals. Sue W. Chapman and Michael Rupured (2014) of the University of Georgia Cooperative Extension find that when people learn time-management skills through self-evaluation and planning, they report that they feel less stress, are more productive, complete more tasks, relate more positively to others, and feel better about themselves while accomplishing the things they want. Mastering resource-management skills not only enhances one's personal life but can contribute substantially to one's effectiveness as an employee. In fact, according to the College and Career Readiness and Success Center (2016), Georgia's employability-skills standards for all career, technical, and agricultural education (CTAE) courses identify time management as a work-readiness trait required for success in the workplace.

Effective time management is not simply about reducing the number of tasks; it's about identifying the appropriate amount of time needed to accomplish a task. Learning how to prioritize personal tasks and activities results in a better balance among school, work, and social lives. Instruction on time management should coincide with discussions about stress. Certainly not all stress can be resolved by exercising time-management skills, but proper time management is one significant way to mitigate stress because it's something over which students have some level of control. Teaching students how to cope with stress is important because, as the Mayo Clinic (2019) reports, unnecessary stress can lead to health issues, including headaches, insomnia, fatigue, muscle tension, and chest pain, which in turn affect mood and behavior. Students' feeling overwhelmed and restless may result in angry outbursts; overeating or undereating; or drug, alcohol, or tobacco use (Mayo Clinic, 2019). As a teacher, you must address the issue of stress in students. While life may be stressful for students now, their level of responsibility only increases in adulthood. Your students need to understand what stress is, what causes it, and how to manage it. Developing time-management skills and healthy coping mechanisms to deal with stressors will make them more-productive students and employees.

Before they can work on time-management skills and coping mechanisms, students need to identify which things they can control and which things they cannot control. Often, students, especially young students, blame themselves for things they cannot control. For example, students have no control over whether their parents divorce or the family relocates because of parents' job opportunities, but students can control whether they are ready in time for school or finish their chores. As an educator, you can foster better time-management skills among your students by encouraging them to do the following.

- Prepare in advance. Make a to-do list, and check off tasks as you complete them. Some find that keeping a running list throughout the day works best. Others find that jotting down a to-do list before going to bed is useful.

- Prioritize assignments and events, and try to estimate the amount of time you'll need to allocate to each of them. Be sure to schedule time for activities that make you happy. Doing things that make you happy is an excellent way to reduce stress.

- Evaluate what you are doing. Consider which tasks are the most important or urgent and whether you are spending too much time scrolling through Instagram, binge-watching shows on Netflix, gaming, and so forth.

- Organize. Everything needs a space, and you may find that a degree of disorganization is causing you to spend your time unproductively, searching for electronic files, handouts, pencils, and the like.

- Break down each item. If you feel overwhelmed by a particular task, remember to take it one step at a time. For example, if you must read an assigned book by the end of the week, try reading a chapter or more here and there, whenever you have a bit of free time, instead of tackling the book all in one go.

Helping students structure time to be more productive is critical, as is recommending strategies for stress management, such as deep breathing, journaling, and activities that involve physical movement and serve to give the brain a break. A simple technique we find beneficial in helping students manage their stress is giving them chewy candy prior to a test; according to professor of psychology Andrew P. Smith (2016), the physical act of chewing helps reduce tension and has a calming effect on the test takers. Teachers can also assist with stress reduction through the way they design their classrooms and structure their lessons. Do not just assign boring seatwork. Let students hear, see, and experience the lessons. Engage your students. Possible strategies for engagement include presenting material through a gallery walk, scavenger hunt, or escape room.

Engagement is strengthened when students take ownership of their learning. One way to facilitate this is by including a service-learning component in the curriculum. Service learning is an excellent way to introduce students to community agencies and the resources that the agencies have available to individuals and families in need of services. But note that service learning is different from community service. Community service is an action—for instance, volunteering for a cause, collecting items for a donation drive, picking up trash, clearing a trail at a state park, or doing bell ringing during the holidays—whereas service learning is an experience and is tied to encouraging academic learning, empowering student voices, and having students practice decision-making skills. With service learning, student involvement includes identifying and researching a problem; using knowledge, skills, and time to find solutions; implementing a plan; taking action; and evaluating the work. It is a powerful teaching tool that supports students' civic engagement and their participation in meaningful and often personally relevant service activities. For example, one of our students organized a successful Relay for Life event after her grandfather passed away following a battle with cancer. She then continued her outreach in college and went back to help even after graduation.

What other practices might fall under the umbrella of service learning? Not just any practice or model will do, as it must meet established service-learning standards of quality. The National Youth Leadership Council (2008a) provides the following standards for service learning in grades K–12: meaningful service, link to curriculum, reflection, diversity, youth voice, partnerships, progress monitoring, and duration and intensity. Table 5.1 features the National Youth Leadership Council's (2008a) definitions of those standards.

Table 5.1: K–12 Service-Learning Standards for Quality Practice

Service-Learning Standard for Quality Practice	Definition
Meaningful Service	Service learning actively engages participants in meaningful and personally relevant service activities.
Link to Curriculum	Service learning is intentionally used as an instructional strategy to meet learning goals or content standards.
Reflection	Service learning incorporates multiple challenging reflection activities that are ongoing and that prompt deep thinking and analysis about oneself and one's relationship to society.

continued ▶

Service-Learning Standard for Quality Practice	Definition
Diversity	Service learning promotes understanding of diversity and mutual respect among all participants.
Youth Voice	Service learning provides students with a strong voice in planning, implementing, and evaluating service-learning experiences with guidance from adults.
Partnerships	Service-learning partnerships are collaborative and mutually beneficial and address community needs.
Progress Monitoring	Service learning engages participants in an ongoing process to assess the quality of implementation and progress toward meeting specified goals and uses results for improvement and sustainability.
Duration and Intensity	Service learning has sufficient duration and intensity to address community needs and meet specified outcomes.

Source: Adapted from National Youth Leadership Council, 2008a.

Quality service learning can fit into your subject matter and curriculum. Implementation is easier in some subjects than in others, but the planning time is worth the effort, as service learning encompasses the spectrum of resource management. Students apply the knowledge they gain through research, network and communicate with experts in the field, identify personal talents and abilities, and consider time and other resources before solidifying a workable plan. The knowledge and skills students acquire through service-learning experiences easily transfer to the workplace. Service learning is powerful because students decide. They partner. They plan. They work. They reflect. They evaluate. They are engaged.

Relay

Throughout adulthood, students will allocate resources in their personal lives and in the workplace. Understanding the value of their available resources and knowing how to manage those resources are important skills to develop and utilize on their journeys. In this section, you will find four activities that will allow your students to practice resource management.

ALLOCATING RESOURCES

This activity consists of five tasks for small groups of students to complete. The goal is for groups to leverage and allocate their resources, in the form of the time available and individuals' knowledge and skills, to complete the tasks.

Materials

Each group of students will need the following.

- A copy of the allocating-resources activity chart (figure 5.1, page 61)
- 1 or 2 stopwatches, depending on the group size
- A simple puzzle (such as a printed maze or a jigsaw puzzle of twenty-four or fewer pieces)
- A brainteaser
- Notebook paper
- Pencils
- A large piece of construction paper
- Markers
- A sudoku puzzle

Directions

To carry out the activity with students, follow these steps.

1. Before students arrive to class, set up the classroom with designated spaces for them to do the following five tasks.

   a. Complete a simple puzzle.

   b. Complete a brainteaser.

   c. Use notebook paper and a pencil to write a ten-line song, rap, or poem that details ways to land a first job.

   d. Use construction paper and markers to create the ultimate employee, illustrating a fictional character who exhibits characteristics of a great employee.

   e. Complete a sudoku puzzle.

2. Once students arrive, divide the class into small groups (four to six students per group, depending on class size).

3. Explain to students that they are now in a workplace setting and each group is competing for a promotion. Tell them that in order to achieve the promotion, as a group, they must complete a series of tasks that will

require them to allocate their individual resources accordingly, choosing the best person for each task to be most efficient. Each student should be assigned to at least one task.

4. Allow students five to ten minutes to divide up the tasks and record on the allocating-resources activity chart (figure 5.1) who will be completing each task and the estimated time it will take to complete the task. The group should aim to pair tasks and group members so that group members can demonstrate their strengths. For each task, if need be, the assigned person can call on a friend from the group to help complete the task. Each group will need one or two stopwatches to record the time taken to accomplish each task, and you can organize the activity according to group size. For example, if there are four students per group, one student may carry out a task at a station, another student will serve as his or her timekeeper, and the remaining two members will watch, waiting either to jump in if called on for help and to record the time once the task is complete. If there are six students per group, you may decide to start two members at different stations, each with his or her own timekeeper. Once a student completes the task and another has recorded his or her time, the student passes the stopwatch, serving as the baton, to another group member, which continues the relay of task completion.

5. Keep track of the order in which the groups finish; however, the emphasis should be on the process, the strategy, and what students learn, rather than on who wins. When everyone is finished, have the group members reflect on the resource-management activity by discussing the following questions.

    a. What would your group do differently if you were to complete this activity again?

    b. What is at least one thing that went well for your group during this activity?

    c. Were you able to correctly gauge how long it would take to complete each task?

    d. What skills did you or your group use in this activity that would be valuable for an employee to have in the workplace?

6. Have each group briefly report out to the class. Following activities with this step reinforces the lesson while continuing to strengthen other employability skills, such as communication and collaboration.

Task	Group Members to Complete the Task	Estimated Time It Will Take	Actual Time Taken
Simple Puzzle			
Brainteaser			
Ten-Line Song, Rap, or Poem			
Ultimate Employee			
Sudoku Puzzle			

Figure 5.1: Allocating-resources activity chart.

*Visit **go.SolutionTree.com/21stcenturyskills** for a free reproducible version of this figure.*

Homestretch

This activity allows for individuals in each group to identify their strengths and use their unique resources to complete the tasks. Often, during the activity, you will see group members volunteering to help one another when participants start to struggle with certain tasks. While strengthening student relationships through team building, the activity offers students a nice introduction to the idea of resource allocation and just how relevant this skill is in any chosen profession.

SCAVENGER HUNT

This scavenger-hunt activity provides a fun approach to reinforce the importance of resource management. This activity produces a lot of noise and movement, but this enjoyment and engagement will support the learning objectives associated with resource management, as the activity emphasizes individual skills, time management, and task prioritization. If your administrator doesn't like noise, use this activity at your own discretion.

Materials

Each group of students will need the following.

- 1 copy of the scavenger-hunt task list (figure 5.2, page 62)
- Scavenger-hunt supplies: blank name tags, crayons, pencils, tape, pieces of paper, and index cards
- A computer or tablet

1. As a group, walk five laps around the classroom. (5 points)

2. Create something for the instructor to wear, such as a hat or a tie. (10 points; 5 bonus points if the instructor actually wears it)

3. Find out something unique about each person in the group, and write down those things on the following lines. (5 points)

   a. _____   d. _____

   b. _____   e. _____

   c. _____

4. Sing "Twinkle, Twinkle, Little Star" together. (15 points)

5. Make a paper airplane, and throw it from one end of the room to the other. (10 points)

6. Get everyone in the room to sign a single piece of paper. (20 points)

7. Count the number of pets owned by your group, and write the number down on the following line. (5 points)

   _____

8. Assign a school-appropriate nickname to each group member, and write down those nicknames on the following lines. (5 points)

   a. _____   d. _____

   b. _____   e. _____

   c. _____

9. Fill out a name tag for each group member. (5 points; 5 bonus points if you use your group nicknames)

10. Build a tower using twenty index cards. (10 points)

11. Convince a member of another group to join your group. (20 points)

12. Name your group, and come up with a group slogan. (5 points for the name; 5 points for the slogan)

    a. Group name: _____

    b. Group slogan: _____

13. Recreate the sounds of the Amazon rain forest using your voices. (5 points)

14. List five things your group has learned about resource management. (15 points)

    a. _____   d. _____

    b. _____   e. _____

    c. _____

15. Form a conga line, and conga from one end of the room to the other. (10 points; 10 bonus points if anyone else joins you)

16. Using your arms, form the initials of your school. (10 points)

17. Find a classmate whose birthday is in January, and record the classmate's name and precise birthday. Repeat this process for each month of the year. A classmate can be on your immediate team or another team. (12 points possible, or 1 point for every birthday recorded)

    a. January: _____   g. July: _____

    b. February: _____   h. August: _____

    c. March: _____   i. September: _____

    d. April: _____   j. October: _____

    e. May: _____   k. November: _____

    f. June: _____   l. December: _____

18. List five colleges in your state or province. (5 points)

    a. _____   d. _____

    b. _____   e. _____

    c. _____

19. Take turns introducing yourselves to and shaking hands with the instructor. (5 points)

20. Have one group member play tic-tac-toe on the whiteboard with someone from another group. (10 points for the winner; 5 points for the loser)

21. At the front of the classroom, dance as a group to "Macarena." You will need to find the song using your tablet or computer. (15 points)

22. Google the Occupational Outlook Handbook, and write down the top five fastest-growing occupations. (10 points)

    a. _____   d. _____

    b. _____   e. _____

    c. _____

23. List three different clubs you could join at school. (5 points)

    a. _____

    b. _____

    c. _____

24. Take a group selfie with a funny poster, figurine, or picture in the classroom. (10 points)

25. Draw on a piece of paper a "turkey family," with group members each outlining one of their hands to represent a turkey. Decorate or dress up each turkey, and create a scene for the turkey family to live in, making sure to use at least five different colors in your picture. Present your artwork to the instructor. (10 points)

Total points: _____

Figure 5.2: Scavenger-hunt task list.

*Visit **go.SolutionTree.com/21stcenturyskills** for a free reproducible version of this figure.*

Directions

To carry out the activity with students, follow these steps.

1. Before students arrive to class, determine who will be in each group of five to six students. Arrange the scavenger-hunt supplies on a table in the classroom for student groups to access. If cell phones are not allowed in the classroom, eliminate item 24 from the scavenger-hunt task list.

2. Be sure that each group has a computer or tablet to use.

3. Allow forty-five minutes to an hour of class time for students to complete the activity. Or rather, the example in this book allows for five minutes of planning, thirty minutes for the activity, and fifteen minutes for wrap-up, though the time allotment can vary depending on the length of your class. But you will want to have ten to fifteen minutes to tally points and facilitate class reflection of the activity; the amount of time you give for actual task completion can be lengthened or shortened without impacting the learning objectives.

4. When the students arrive, divide the class into predetermined groups. Verbally provide an overview of the activity rules that follow (though you may also wish to display the rules on a flip chart or whiteboard), and pass out the task-list sheets.

    a. Groups will have five minutes to plan and thirty minutes to complete as many tasks as possible.

    b. Groups must complete each task as a team. During the planning time, each group will decide the order of the tasks, whether they think a leader is needed for a task, and who the leader or leaders will be.

    c. Supplies to complete the tasks are on a table at the front of the room.

    d. No outside supplies may be used (except for a cell phone for a selfie if item 24 remains on the task list).

    e. One team member will be the recorder and fill in the task-list sheet when needed, mark off completed tasks, and circle the score the team earns for each task. The group with the most points at the end is the winner.

Homestretch

Discuss the point of the scavenger hunt and how it relates to resource management. Have the students consider how this activity and the learning objectives—participants' planning, delegating, and dividing time to achieve different tasks—could apply to their daily lives. Examine how leadership was used to complete specific tasks. What went into the decision-making process—the point value of the tasks or ability to complete tasks? After students reflect on the strategies and skills they used to complete the tasks, transfer the learning to employability skills; ask students, "How do the skills you used in the activity apply to being a contributing member of the workforce?"

IT'S ABOUT TIME

This activity will help you prove to your students the importance of planning and delegating tasks and effectively managing time. Each group member is to work as efficiently as possible to complete the three rounds of the task, and groups compete against one another to finish the task first. This fun, competitive activity will surely get everyone energized and motivated.

Materials

For this activity, you'll need access to the following.

- A computer with PowerPoint and an LCD projector

- 1 deck of cards per group

- 1 stopwatch or cell phone with a stopwatch app per group, plus 1 for yourself

Directions

To carry out the activity with students, follow these steps.

1. Before students arrive to class, create a PowerPoint slide of figure 5.3 (page 66) and a slide of the activity rules listed in step 2. Prepare to allow twenty-five minutes for the activity.

2. When the students arrive, divide the class into groups of four to five students, and distribute the materials to each group. Pull up the PowerPoint slide of the activity rules, and review them with the class.

   a. You must lay out the cards exactly as shown on the slide.

   b. All cards must be in tidy rows, with no cards touching.

   c. You will have a two-minute practice round, which I will time.

   d. After the practice round, I'll set my timer for three minutes, during which your team should develop a strategy for the next round.

   e. For rounds one, two, and three, a member of the team will use a stopwatch or cell phone to keep track of the time. Time will begin when I say *go* and will stop when your team has completed the task. Note that taking cell phone pictures is not allowed.

3. Show the PowerPoint slide of figure 5.3, and initiate the practice round. After the practice round, allow students their three minutes of planning time. Once students have planned and shuffled their cards, initiate the first round. Teams will finish at different times and will need to record their times.

4. When the last team finishes round one, remove the card-layout slide from view. Check students' work, making sure lines are straight and no cards are touching. Have groups shuffle their cards. Reveal the card-layout slide, initiate round two, and repeat the preceding process for rounds two and three.

5. After round three, have each group share with the class their times and the strategic adjustments they made from round to round. Did their time improve? If so, why? If not, can they identify now what they should have done differently?

♣		A	5	K	2	8	4	7	J	6	10	Q	3	9
♦		A	5	K	2	8	4	7	J	6	10	Q	3	9
♠		A	5	K	2	8	4	7	J	6	10	Q	3	9
♥		A	5	K	2	8	4	7	J	6	10	Q	3	9

Figure 5.3: Card layout for the PowerPoint slide.

Visit **go.SolutionTree.com/21stcenturyskills** *for a free reproducible version of this figure.*

Homestretch

With this activity, students typically don't start with a great strategy during the practice round. Then, during the following rounds, they begin strategizing, dividing the work among the group members, and significantly improving the group's time. The main takeaway from this activity is that devising a solid plan at the outset will help eliminate confusion and misdirected effort.

SERVICE-LEARNING PROJECT

To give students the background that they will need to complete this activity, explain to students that sometimes local agencies need assistance collecting resources and they turn to community members for help. Then pose the following questions: "Why might people need help from a community agency? What agencies in our community might need our support? Where should we look to find out more about the agencies our community has to offer?" These questions serve as a lead-in to discussing potential service-learning projects, but they also educate your students on community resources and how they might go about finding resources they may need now or in the future.

Depending on students' interests, you can set up service-learning opportunities for individual students, student partners, small groups, or the entire class. Please note that you and the class do not determine how to help; experts from agencies share what their organizations need.

As the classroom instructor, you can set parameters for the amount of time that students dedicate to a service-learning project, as well as for the types of projects from which they should choose. This way, you can ensure their projects closely align to your subject matter. But note that in order for their service-learning projects to be meaningful, students must ultimately determine the project specifics; their projects must be something they want to do.

Materials

Each student will need the following.

- 1 service-learning completion sheet (figure 5.4, page 68)
- 1 pen or pencil

Directions

To carry out the activity with students, follow these steps.

1. As preparation, research to find various local community agencies in need of assistance. Some larger communities have volunteer networks through which agencies post specific needs.

2. Decide on the amount of classroom time students should devote to service learning. For the most-effective service learning, the National Youth Leadership Council (2008a) recommends a duration of several weeks or months, but hours can come from in-school and out-of-school time. This time estimation includes all project components, from researching and planning to providing the service. However, this time doesn't all need to be spent during class. Students should work on various components on their own time for efficiency's and practicality's sake.

Project Leader: _____

Group Members: _____

Project Name: _____

Investigate

Does this project meet a real community need? (Circle yes or no.)

Yes   No

Can you find a community partner to help you? (Circle yes or no.)

Yes   No

If yes, who?

How will you collaborate with your community partner?

What problems or needs has the community partner identified?

What problem or need will you target for your service project?

How did you identify this as a need? (Check all that apply.)

☐ Through personal observations, experiences, or passions

☐ By developing and conducting a survey

☐ By conducting interviews

☐ By talking to the community partner

☐ By doing research through consulting books, documents, websites, or videos

☐ Other

Who is your target audience?

Research the problem, and write a summary of your research, including statistics to justify the problem as a need. Investigate local, state, national, and global statistics. What are the relevant facts you would want to share with others?

Prepare and Plan

Project goal or goals:

Describe the project (in seventy-five words or fewer).

What are the logistics of your project?

- Project date: _____
- Project time: _____
- Location: _____
- Equipment: _____
- Budget: _____
- Supplies: _____
- Estimated cost of supplies: _____

Will you require transportation to the project site? (Circle yes or no.)

Yes   No

If yes, how will you be transported?

How will you be supervised (that is, by whom)?

Can you complete the project within the given time frame? (Circle yes or no.)

Yes   No

Who will be the official project photographer or videographer and document the process?

How will you advertise or publicize the project?

What social media platforms will you use? (Circle all that apply.)

Instagram   Twitter   Facebook   Other

What do you need to do to prepare for the project?

Figure 5.4: Service-learning completion sheet.

continued ▶

How will you divide the work responsibilities for the project? (Fill out the following table with this information.)

Group Member	Responsibilities

Will this project have a visible or obvious result? (Circle yes or no.)

Yes   No

If yes, please describe it.

How will you measure the success of your project?

What baseline data will you use for comparison to determine the impact of your project?

Create a Project Impact Report

Individually, complete a reflection on the project. Address the following questions.

- What did you learn about your topic?
- Why was the project important? What difference did it make?
- What was your personal involvement in the project—your strengths and weaknesses?
- What were the successes and disappointments of the project?
- What would be your do-overs if you had the opportunity to complete the project again?
- In a sentence or two, how would you summarize the success of the project or event, including the impact, awareness, and responses among community members?
- What sorts of feedback did you receive from community members?

Create a Group Impact Report

What was the scale of the project (its number of participants)?

Did you meet the goals of the project? (Refer to your preparation details.)

What impact did your work have on the school, the community, or individuals? (How did it change your school or community?)

What is the project's measure of success? (Compare the baseline data you collected at the beginning of the project through research, observations, or surveys to the outcome data to see what impact your group made.)

Demonstrate and Celebrate

Take the following steps when the project is complete.

1. Report out to the class on the project, including accomplishments, do-overs, and what you learned. Be sure to include details on scale, impact, and measure of success.

2. Submit at least one photo and media release of the project to a local newspaper or school publication. Attach a copy of the email or article to this form.

3. Send thank-you notes to all community partners, sponsors, and volunteers. Be sure to include city and county officials, school personnel, and other school and community resources.

Source: Adapted from Youth Service America, n.d.
*Visit **go.SolutionTree.com/21stcenturyskills** for a free reproducible version of this figure.*

3. To begin implementing service learning, as a class, make a list of situations or issues that individuals and families may face for which they would need help (for example, job loss, homelessness, drug abuse, child neglect or abuse, food deserts, domestic violence, and so forth).

4. From the list, have students identify possible organizations and agencies that could assist with those situations or issues.

5. Have students decide which issue they want to further research. Each student will need to also decide whether he or she wishes to work alone or as a member of a group.

6. Have students—whether working alone, in pairs, or in small groups—use the service-learning completion sheet (figure 5.4, page 68) to work through the steps of creating a service-learning project. Ask that they be mindful of certain constraints, such as time, budget, and transportation. Note, however, that you as the instructor will need to set the larger parameters. For example, most classrooms will not have a budget with which to purchase supplies. Some schools will not allow field trips or cover the cost of transportation for a field trip. Provide such relevant details to students so they can consider them as they develop their plans.

7. Help students keep track of their service-learning project hours, as these details can help students meet graduation requirements, enhance their college applications, build résumés, strengthen job applications, and tackle future goals. In Indiana, for example, service learning meets a Graduation Pathways requirement.

Homestretch

Service learning is a teaching tool that blends academic learning with action taking. It provides students with concrete opportunities to make decisions, execute plans they've crafted, and develop a keen awareness and deep understanding of community support systems. Through student-led projects, students learn not only how to plan, organize, and implement but how to evaluate their work. Students of the 21st century have a real concern for others, and they want to make a difference. As a teacher and facilitator, you will help your students realize how individual effort can effect change, and they'll learn where to go if they need help in the future.

Conclusion

Resource management encompasses knowing how to distribute resources efficiently and effectively. Educators must work to ensure that their students participate in relevant scenarios to practice competent ways to complete tasks. Learning how to prioritize and how to allot time to finish tasks is foundational—so, too, are practice and repetition, as they encourage proficiency in resource management. Help students recognize the importance of using their time wisely, and share practical strategies for successfully completing tasks. Not just productivity is at stake; with poor planning and time management comes undue personal stress. During the study of resource management, students should work through various activities that demonstrate the direct effects of optimum time-management skills and show that they can exert greater control over their responsibilities by breaking down each of their to-do items into manageable chunks. Finally, using service learning as a teaching tool introduces students to community resources; reinforces other employability skills (such as teamwork and collaboration, communication, and critical thinking and problem solving); and truly empowers students, as they learn firsthand the difference they can make in the world by using their employability skills.

CHAPTER 6

Growth Mindset, Resilience, and Grit

Throughout their personal and professional journeys, students must nurture within themselves a healthy, productive mindset and commit to lifelong learning. From the educational realm, mindset transfers to and affects outcomes in personal relationships, athletics, leadership, and career advancement, among other things, and is even reflected in company philosophies, according to psychologist Carol S. Dweck (2016).

What exactly is mindset? *Mindset* refers to self-perception of one's intelligence, abilities, and talents, and Dweck (2016) specifies that one's mindset can fall into one of two classifications: (1) growth mindset or (2) fixed mindset. And only growth mindset encompasses many of the traits that lead to success. A person with a growth mindset believes that people grow and develop skills and intelligence—that individuals are in control of their skills and abilities. In contrast, a person with a fixed mindset believes skills and intelligence are innate and individuals therefore have little control over their abilities (Dweck, 2016). The good news is that people can intentionally shift their mindset with awareness and a desire to change.

Promoting resilience against adversity is the natural complement to teaching mindset. Many of your students face deleterious situations in their day-to-day lives. And as Joshua D. Margolis, the head of organizational behavior at Harvard Business School, and Paul G. Stoltz (2010), developer of the Adversity Quotient theory, write, these students may be experiencing feelings of helplessness, confusion, discouragement, and anger. Negative emotions can stifle people in the moment and prevent them from moving on and flourishing. Coaching students on how to counter adversity with resilience and what psychologist Angela Duckworth (2016) calls *grit*—a combination of perseverance and passion—shifts focus to a forward-thinking mindset.

A growth mindset, resilience, and grit are personal attributes that will serve students well in their everyday lives and in the workforce. Organizations want employees who possess a willingness to learn and a can-do attitude—people who view obstacles as rewarding challenges and who power through them with persistence. Employers need individuals who can bounce back from situations with resolve. Let's explore the rationale behind promoting a growth mindset, resilience, and grit; the research that supports this skill set's relevance in the workforce; and activities that will help facilitate this skill development in students.

Rationale

Educators must understand that, although students might not realize it, their past experiences impact their mindsets, and introducing the concept of mindset to students allows them to better self-reflect and self-assess. Researcher Betsy Ng (2018) explains that academic achievement, engagement, and a willingness to take on new, unfamiliar tasks are related to having a growth mindset. The work of Dweck (2016) and Yeager and colleagues (2019), too, shows that growth mindset interventions positively impact young people, especially those who face challenges. As a teacher, you must reinforce the idea that each student can learn and grow by striving toward a growth mindset.

In reviewing the activities in this book, you may have noticed that they often have no right answer, or no single right answer; 100 percent student engagement is ideal; and learning is more about the process than about the outcome. This is not coincidental but rather purposeful, because the educational system has suppressed many students—those who, for example, may begin in a lower-level reading group in elementary school, receive Fs on numerous papers, and perform poorly on achievement tests. Continually, these students endure interventions and remediations that check on improvement gains. These situations may convey to students, "You're not good enough," which takes a toll on their self-concept and self-esteem and leads to a fixed mindset.

The reverse scenario may also be the norm—yet still result in a fixed mindset. Students who are in a higher-level reading group, receive straight As on their report cards, and score high on achievement tests may struggle with their self-perception when a challenging situation presents itself and they are no longer on top. They may shut down or succumb to a give-up attitude. We have observed this with students at the top of their class who go to college and drop out within the first year or who decide not to take a higher-level mathematics class for fear of getting a grade lower than an A. They feel great discomfort in a challenging situation, or at the prospect of not being recognized as one of the best, which fuels a fixed mindset. To encourage a growth mindset in students, teachers must offer a variety of activities and opportunities for success and illustrate to students how to approach challenges and setbacks as learning opportunities rather than as threats to their intelligence and abilities. In particular, according to Carol S. Dweck, Gregory M. Walton, and Geoffrey L. Cohen (2014), learning activities in cooperative environments improve student success and motivation, as they eliminate the component of competition.

Some students meet life challenges with resilience and grit, while others need support and additional resources to do this. Common types of adversity include abuse (physical, sexual, or verbal), neglect (lack of food, clothing, or safety), addiction, mental-health disorders, domestic violence, neighborhood violence, poverty, financial hardship, homelessness, divorce, incarceration of a family member, chronic illness, physical limitations, and academic limitations. Examining findings from a survey of multiple countries across five continents, Robert W. Blum (2019), professor at Johns Hopkins Bloomberg School of Public Health, reveals "46% of young adolescents reported experiencing violence, 38% suffered emotional neglect and 29% experienced physical neglect," often leading to depression and violent actions. When you are aware of such issues among your students, you may feel it's an uphill battle to teach them about having a growth mindset, or about the importance of resilience and grit, but really, this is when students most need this instruction. You must help your students successfully navigate the turbulence.

We love "the power of *yet*" (Dweck, 2014) and its valuable role in teaching about mindset. The power of *yet* communicates that students' first try may not produce their intended outcome and that repeated failures may occur before they master the task at hand. Students need to realize that just because a person can't do something *yet*, it doesn't mean the person can't do it. For instance, test scores may indicate where students are but not where they will end up. You might reinforce the concept for students by reminding them that everyone has had to practice to learn something— dancing a routine, casting a fishing lure, showing animals at a fair, riding a bicycle, reciting the alphabet, playing on a sports team, and so on. Emphasize the power of *yet*: "I can't do it yet" instead of simply "I can't do it."

Lessons on the power of *yet* should include a real acknowledgment of those repeated failures along the way. As a teacher, you'll often see students who appear to have broken spirits. Helping to repair broken spirits, while not necessarily part of the teacher's job description, is often the most treasured gift you can give your students. In teaching about resilience and grit, reference notable figures who overcame adversity to achieve their goals and dreams. To start a discussion, cite a variety of people with different talents—for example, Adam Levine, Buzz Aldrin, Toni Morrison, Michael J. Fox, Stevie Wonder, Stephen King, Jennifer Lopez, Demi Lovato, and Albert Einstein. Be sure to include entrepreneurs who failed, and some who failed repeatedly, such as Walt Disney, Soichiro Honda, Colonel Sanders, Steven Spielberg, Arianna Huffington,

Vera Wang, and Milton Hershey. (Your students will likely happily add to the list.) These well-known figures were resilient and did not let difficult circumstances or other people dictate their futures. Impress on your students that grit is a time-tested way to approach future dreams.

But students should be aware that grit and resilience aren't just reserved for their loftier ambitions, of course; these qualities are practical and necessary for day-to-day life. Whether students transition into postsecondary education or immediately enter the workforce, setbacks and changes will be a reality. How students deal with learning new skills and with receiving feedback can impact their chances of advancing in their careers and finding happiness in their work. Offering students the chance to practice competencies with a not-yet attitude in a controlled environment builds their self-assurance. And as an educator, you want to instill the idea that learning is a lifelong process—and through persistence and effort comes success.

Research

Dweck's (2016) work will be foundational as you introduce your students to the concept of mindset. And in another invaluable resource, *Poor Students, Rich Teaching*, Eric Jensen (2019) establishes seven *teaching* mindsets that will help you build successful relationships with your students, especially those students from poverty: (1) relational mindset, (2) achievement mindset, (3) positivity mindset, (4) rich classroom climate mindset, (5) enrichment mindset, (6) engagement mindset, and (7) graduation mindset. Jensen (2019) deeply understands poverty, and from the start of his book, he provides teachers with the tools to connect to students as individuals; "always connect first as a person (and an ally) and second as a teacher," he writes (p. 11). His research supports the idea that classroom relationships are indicators of whether students will drop out of school as much as IQs or test scores are (Jensen, 2019). If a teacher doesn't have a growth mindset toward learning and accomplishment, how can the teacher facilitate a growth mindset in students?

Working on your own mindset as you support the development of healthy mindsets among your students is all well and good. But in addition to explicitly communicating to students the importance of a growth mindset against the backdrop of educational goal setting, for example, you'll need to be able to answer students' inevitable *why*: "Why do we need to work so hard on changing our mindsets?" Luckily, the real-world ramifications are unmistakable. According to the World Economic Forum (2020a), the Fourth Industrial Revolution is creating emerging professions that require skill sets for keeping up with ever-advancing technology in addition to maintaining interpersonal relationships—providing direct care or services to others. You can better prepare your students for these and future careers that are nonexistent today by first incorporating employability skills into your daily lessons and promoting a mindset through which students will be persistent in the face of challenges and quick to take initiative. Equip your students with critical-thinking, problem-solving, and teamwork skills, as well as social skills, persistence, and creativity—those, according to economist Emma Garcia (2014), should be pillars in education. Teaching *employability skills*, *soft skills*, *professional skills*, or *noncognitive skills*—whatever term you prefer to use—will lead to improved academic success for your students, and the skills will transfer into various aspects of their adult lives.

To emphasize the importance of being resilient, look to the workplace for examples that support this learning in your classroom. Provisional psychologist Heather Craig (2020) writes that resilience is a skill and needs to be practiced just like other skills. Employers often instruct managers on how to be resilient in response to crisis, and Margolis and Stoltz (2010) identify four lenses—(1) control, (2) impact, (3) breadth, and (4) duration—through which managers can view personal and professional challenges or failures and productively respond to them. We can apply these same principles to teaching our students how to fight adversity with resilience. First, we must acknowledge that feeling a sense of defeat and taking a situation personally are normal emotional responses. But what happens next is a choice to change one's mindset. Margolis and Stoltz (2010) state that resilient managers quickly move to a plan of action, identifying how to improve or influence the situation (control), what actions will have the most positive effects (impact), how to contain and alter the situation (breadth), and what actions can be implemented to get past the hardship (duration). Margolis and Stoltz (2010) add that managers should not give pep talks but encourage an inquisitive approach to help employees come up with their own options and possibilities for solutions—we want to do the same for our students as we build resilient learners.

Of course, we cannot discuss grit without further exploring Duckworth's (2016) extensive work on the topic. Duckworth notes that effort often outweighs talent because of the grit that can accompany one's effort. Through her research, she finds that when hiring a new employee, an employer is nearly five times more likely to choose effort and hard work over talent and intelligence than vice versa (Duckworth, 2016). In terms of the classroom context, she writes that a struggling student may just need extra time to master a concept. When a student struggles, it's up to the classroom teacher to make a choice: Should the teacher be quick to judge and grade performance? Or should that teacher promote grit by placing value on effort and practice and encouraging the student to gain mastery? Your students need to understand that grit can grow through practicing and pursuing interests. If you help your students develop grit, you'll nourish hope, instill a sense of purpose, and encourage effort toward a better tomorrow.

Relay

To better understand growth mindset, resilience, and grit, students need to practice self-reflection and analyze how they approach obstacles and challenges. In this section, you'll find activities that foster greater comprehension of these topics, promote personal reflection, and provide opportunities for groups to reflect and share.

POSITIVE SELF-TALK AND SELF-AFFIRMATION

Let's start with a simple activity for your students. Practicing positive self-talk and self-affirmation can help students develop a positive self-concept and put them on a path to cultivating a growth mindset.

Materials

Each student will need the following.

- 1 positive self-talk and self-affirmation worksheet (figure 6.1)

- 1 pen or pencil

What things on this list could you say about yourself? (Check all that apply.)

☐ I am a good friend.

☐ I am creative.

☐ I am kind and loved.

☐ I am capable of anything.

☐ With effort and determination, I can succeed.

☐ I have a caring heart.

☐ I am forgiving.

☐ I am grateful.

☐ I am beautiful inside and out.

☐ I am proud of myself.

☐ When I practice, I see positive results.

☐ I might not know something *yet*, but that doesn't mean I won't know it in the future.

☐ I will pass all my classes and earn all my potential credits this year.

☐ My failures can lead to my success.

☐ My potential is limitless.

Figure 6.1: Positive self-talk and self-affirmation worksheet.

*Visit **go.SolutionTree.com/21stcenturyskills** for a free reproducible version of this figure.*

Directions

To carry out the activity with students, follow these steps.

1. Distribute the worksheet (figure 6.1) to students, and tell them to complete it.

2. Explain to the students what a self-affirmation is—a statement that affirms your worthiness—and that writing one down helps it become

part of your being. Some people write self-affirmations and goals on their bathroom mirrors with dry-erase markers, on pillowcases with fabric markers, or on sticky notes they can leave in different locations. Simply putting the positive messages out there can help make them a reality and eliminate self-doubt with a "Yes, I can" attitude.

3. Instruct students to write down one goal they have for themselves for the next month or so. Tell them they shouldn't make it so far out of reach that it takes too long to see results. Examples might include passing an upcoming test or exercising three times a week. Students should practice a growth-mindset attitude and have the goal visible so that they can see it every day, perhaps writing it on an agenda they use every day, setting it as their phone's home screen, or creating a vision board or goal poster.

Homestretch

Why incorporate this type of activity? Positive self-talk and self-affirmations build confidence. We want our students to embrace the power of *yet* and comprehend that, with intentional effort and perseverance, they can achieve. And goal setting should become part of students' lives, giving them a sense of direction—a way to work through challenges to make an aspiration become a reality.

GROWTH MINDSET VERSUS FIXED MINDSET

This activity provides a quick check for understanding of the concept of growth mindset and its significance.

Materials

For this activity, you'll need the following.

-   A computer with PowerPoint and an LCD projector
-   A slide presentation featuring the growth-mindset-versus-fixed-mindset statements (see figure 6.2, page 82)

Directions

To carry out the activity with students, follow these steps.

1. Display for students the slide presentation featuring the ten growth-mindset-versus-fixed-mindset statements (figure 6.2, page 82).

2. Ask students to identify whether each statement displays a growth mindset or a fixed mindset. Have the students jot down their answers. If you have adequate space in your classroom, designate one side of the room to represent growth mindset and the other fixed mindset, and ask

that students respond by physically moving to the appropriate location. This gets students out of their seats, and if there are different responses, discussion can follow. (Students should identify statements 1, 4, 6, 8, and 10 as those of a growth mindset and statements 2, 3, 5, 7, and 9 as those of a fixed mindset.)

Directions:

Identify whether each statement that follows displays a growth mindset or a fixed mindset.

1. It's not that I'm so smart; it's just that I stay with the problem longer.
2. I don't think we will win the game on Friday night; they always beat us.
3. I love fair time and showing livestock, but my animal can never beat that family's animal.
4. I learn more from failure than from success.
5. I just cannot do mathematics.
6. With effort and determination, I can succeed.
7. I have a temper just like my dad, and I can't change that.
8. I can do anything I put my mind to.
9. I really like them, but they would never be interested in knowing me.
10. I haven't mastered it yet.

Figure 6.2: Growth mindset versus fixed mindset.

*Visit **go.SolutionTree.com/21stcenturyskills** for a free reproducible version of this figure.*

Homestretch

Discuss how the mindset may impact the outcome in each of the stated situations. Invite students to reword the fixed-mindset statements so they read as growth-mindset statements.

SELF-REFLECTION

In this activity, journaling allows students to explore their thoughts on mindset, mistakes they've made, challenges they've faced, and personal goals they may not feel comfortable disclosing to the entire class. You can decide if you want the journals to be for their eyes only or if you want to learn more about your students by reviewing their writing. Be sure to let the students know your intent in this regard when you provide directions.

Materials

For this activity, you'll need the following.

- A computer with PowerPoint and an LCD projector
- A slide presentation featuring the self-reflection questions (see figure 6.3)
- 1 piece of paper and 1 pen or pencil per student for written responses

Directions

To carry out the activity with students, follow these steps.

1. Display for students the slide presentation featuring the five self-reflection questions (figure 6.3).

2. Have students each record their responses to the self-reflection questions using their electronic device or their pen or pencil and piece of paper.

Directions:

Answer the following questions.

1. Why is it important to have a growth mindset? Do you think you have one? Depending on your answer, why did you say *yes* or *no*?

2. Think about a mistake you have made. What lessons did you learn from that mistake?

3. What is one of your long-term goals? What are you doing now to achieve it?

4. How can you implement the power of *yet* into your daily life?

5. What will you do to challenge yourself today? This week? This year?

Figure 6.3: Self-reflection questions.

*Visit **go.SolutionTree.com/21stcenturyskills** for a free reproducible version of this figure.*

Homestretch

Self-reflection is a valuable tool to enhance learning. Having students individually reflect and process their thoughts on these questions can give them a deeper understanding of themselves. Sometimes, reflecting starts the thought process, creating a motion before action or change can take place. We recommend this as a journaling activity rather than a group discussion because it allows for privacy of answers and, as a result, more serious, meaningful responses from students.

CHATTER ROCKS

This chatter-rock activity provides talking points for students to share successes and personal struggles along with thoughts on family and friends. The activity allows for students to learn more about their classmates' experiences, often seeing that they have more in common than they previously thought.

Materials

Each group of students will need the following.

- 1 set of chatter rocks (see figure 6.4)
- 1 set of chatter-rock cards (figure 6.5)

Directions

To carry out the activity with students, follow these steps.

1. In preparation for the classroom activity, purchase rocks or stones to create painted chatter rocks as shown in figure 6.4.

2. To begin the activity, divide the class into groups of four to five students.

3. Dole out the sets of chatter rocks and cards.

4. Explain the following activity steps to the students.

   a. Working in your group, lay out the chatter rocks randomly, with the designs or words faceup.

   b. Shuffle the chatter cards (figure 6.5), and lay them facedown in a stack.

   c. Determine who is oldest in the group, and have this group member start by picking up a card and reading it aloud.

   d. All the group members, including the card reader, take turns picking up a chatter rock that in some way supports their personal thoughts on the card and sharing their thoughts with the group.

   e. The person to the left of the oldest member reads the next card, and the process continues until the group goes through the entire stack. (Note that each group member is allowed to pass on answering one question.)

5. Allow students twenty to twenty-five minutes to complete this activity.

Homestretch

The goal of this activity is to get students talking so they realize they are not alone in their daily struggles and their classmates often experience similar situations. From

?	♥	👁 👁
Y	STOP	X
☺	★	🔒
💭	⚡	🚫
Strength	Brave	Freedom
Faith	Family	Time
Friends	Fun	Determined
Balance	Peace	Happy
Hope	Believe	Involvement
Courage	Love	Values
Create	Talent	Graduate

Figure 6.4: Chatter-rock designs.

*Visit **go.SolutionTree.com/21stcenturyskills** for a free reproducible version of this figure.*

Should school become totally virtual, or is face-to-face interaction important in the learning process?	What activities could you take part in that would divert your attention from your smartphone?
When was the last time you did something that scared or challenged you?	What skill could you teach someone else in two minutes?
Would you consider a career that some might view as nontraditional for your gender (for example, doing construction for a woman or teaching preschool for a man)?	What do you want more from a career—happiness or wealth?
What are you looking forward to, or dreading, this school year?	What are you grateful for?
What ideas do you have for enhancing your community?	If you had the power to drop any course from your schedule, what course would you drop?
What role does procrastination play in your life?	How competitive are you?

Figure 6.5: Chatter-rock cards.   continued ▶

What family traditions do you want to carry on as you grow older?	How do you deal with haters?
How often do you leave your comfort zone?	What are your secret survival strategies?
What challenges have you overcome?	How should parents handle a child's failing report card?
Should all students be drug tested?	What superpower do you wish you had?
Should students be able to graduate from high school as soon as they earn the necessary credits and meet established requirements (rather than having to fulfill year-based conditions as well)?	When do you become an adult?
Are you worried about someday becoming addicted to drugs or alcohol?	Do parents have different hopes and standards for their sons than they have for their daughters?
What are some reasons why a student might be failing in school?	How well do you think standardized tests measure your abilities?
Should tablet computers become the primary way students learn in class?	Which is more important—talent or hard work?
What skills are you learning in school that will help you succeed in life?	Can money buy you happiness?
Should schools put tracking devices in students' ID cards?	Does technology make us more alone, and are likes on social media affecting people's self-worth?
What do you need, and what do you want?	What experiences do you think have impacted your life thus far?
What do you wish you knew how to do?	What do you see yourself doing in five years? Ten years?
Do you consider yourself a leader?	Do you think you hold yourself back?

Visit **go.SolutionTree.com/21stcenturyskills** *for a free reproducible version of this figure.*

fun questions such as "What superpower do you wish you had?" to more thought-provoking questions such as "What ideas do you have for enhancing your community?" this activity sets the stage for students to talk, think, and respond to others, creating an opportunity for them to strengthen their communication skills. The activity also opens up discussions on resilience and growth mindset with questions on survival strategies and personal comfort zones. But be judicious about when you introduce this activity, as there should be a basis of trust and a sense of security in the classroom; you want your students not to leave class telling others, "You should have heard what so-and-so said," but rather to have empathy and show support for their peers.

Conclusion

We like to think of our students as being resilient. Many do seem to have an uncanny ability to recover quickly from difficult or negative situations. However, not *all* do, and they may require time, effort, and patience to recover. Teaching students about mindset allows them to evaluate their approach to a variety of situations, and in developing a growth mindset, students gain personal power. The power of *yet* can change their views from "I can't" to "I can't *yet*," and they'll realize that learning a skill often takes practice and repetition. Developing and maintaining a growth mindset is a skill that will benefit them in academics, relationships, business, athletics, music, and so on—impacting today's students and, as a result, tomorrow's workforce. Once students learn to handle tough situations and they develop skills to carry themselves beyond negativity, they'll be able to look past the bumps in the road and continue on their journeys toward personal and professional fulfillment. But remember that it is essential that you, as the teacher, have and showcase a growth mindset as you facilitate your students' learning. You are the role model and the mentor preparing your students to be college and career ready—in fact, *life ready*.

CHAPTER 7

Ethics, Values, and Integrity

Can professional skills that are critical to workplace success really be taught in a classroom setting? The answer is *yes*! Ethics, values, and integrity comprise a set of characteristics that teachers want to instill in their students and employers want to be able to count on in the workplace. According to *Merriam-Webster*, *ethics* refers to "the discipline dealing with what is good and bad and with moral duty and obligation" and "tends to suggest aspects of universal fairness and the question of whether or not an action is responsible" ("Ethics," n.d.). For example, if someone behaves in an ethical manner, people may see him or her as someone who completes an assigned task to the highest standard, makes prudent choices, and follows rules. *Values* encompass principles or qualities that are "intrinsically valuable or desirable" ("Value," n.d.). In the workplace environment, this goes beyond a matter of right and wrong; for example, it's important that a team adheres to a common set of values—such as accountability, respect, and attention to detail—as its members work on a project. This provides the foundation for a sense of trust among members. And as journalist David Weedmark (n.d.) suggests, it's critical that, once managers communicate company values to employees and make it clear they will uphold them themselves, employees take those values to heart and conduct themselves accordingly. When we think about integrity, we consider people's personal morals and ability to act ethically when others are not looking, according to management consultant Susan M. Heathfield (2020). Personally speaking, the level of integrity to which we hold ourselves as educators is precisely what led us to develop our employability-skills framework. We have goals for ourselves and for our students that can be accomplished only through hard work and dedication to meeting specific criteria. Integrity serves as the foundation for our teaching and training the students whose futures we hope include happiness and gainful employment. Likewise, we know that educators worldwide share these hopes and seek to impart characteristics such as ethics, values, and integrity to their students in order to realize these goals. In this chapter, we'll discuss the rationale for embedding ethics, values, and integrity in the classroom; the research that supports this skill set's inclusion in the employability-skills framework; and activities that will get students honing and thinking more deeply about this crucial skill set.

Rationale

Ethics, values, and integrity are critical competencies. Training on adhering to ethical guidelines and upholding integrity in the workplace provides important competencies for model practices across a spectrum of career fields. Whether a student decides to enter into automobile manufacturing or health care, for instance, ethics is a critical piece in the instruction you provide to the student. Think about your car's braking system or airbag installation, or the prescription and dispensation of medication. If ethics and integrity were not valued in the automotive industry, there would be no recalls on defective parts. Ethics in health care provides for a variety of treatment options for illnesses, which are patient centered and not strictly driven by a company's bottom line. It's useful to communicate the importance of these concepts with students by exploring such real-world situations.

The students in our building-construction program have in-depth discussions with their instructor and review Occupational Safety and Health Administration (OSHA) regulations prior to going off-site for a project. In fact, students must complete a ten-hour OSHA training session at the beginning of each school year so that our safety expectations and guidelines for proper construction are unambiguous. Once, at a local school board presentation, a board member had questions about our building-construction program and the specifics regarding how we teach our students ethical guidelines. The discussion ensued because a school board member's friend had recently had repairs completed by a local construction company. Once the repairs were near completion, this person had asked a friend, who happened to be a city inspector, to look at the progress. Much to the inspector's dismay, the repairs did not meet building codes. That left many questions regarding ethics and values in the building-construction arena. Fortunately, we were able to report that we teach students in our building-construction class—actually, in all our programs—code-specific skills, as well as professional skills, including ethics, values, and integrity. Teachers and students spend time talking about decision making in the classroom and on the jobsite regarding the correct materials for specific procedures. Students must analyze the job skills needed to complete a task in a safe, effective manner while maintaining the integrity of best practices from real-world codes of conduct—for example, the lockout-tagout process used in electrical-wiring work on a jobsite, which aids communication among colleagues and prevents injury. In fact, in this case, valuing the correct way to work can be lifesaving.

One specific example in which one of our students was able to demonstrate his ability to maintain an ethical high ground was during an internship with an auto-services dealership. The student had spent his junior year and half of his senior year at Hoosier Hills Career Center training for an internship opportunity. He was nervous about working for a larger dealership, so he requested placement at a smaller shop. We accommodated the request and completed the necessary paperwork for him to begin. After just two weeks, the student came into the center, nervous and upset, and asked to end his internship. Once we assured him he would not have to return to the site, he shared what he had seen. The shop owner would give a customer an estimate and order the necessary part for the vehicle. He would then take the old part off the vehicle and, rather than replace it with the new part, clean the old part, make a minor adjustment, and put it right back on the vehicle. Such parts were still in working order and did not need to be replaced, but this was how the small shop functioned. When the customer returned and explained that the car was acting up again, the shop owner again serviced the vehicle and ordered a part, replaced the old part with the part the customer initially purchased, kept the second part for which the customer paid, and collected money for his time and labor. Our student was so shocked and disappointed by what he saw that he could not return to the shop. He explained that he would never think to do something like that but learned through the troubling experience how *not* to act as an employee. He was able to hold himself to high moral standards despite having seen an adult business owner making such poor choices.

As educators, we are so pleased when students share these types of outcomes with us, and it solidifies our reasoning for prompting students to think more intentionally about what it is they value in themselves and what values they expect of others in personal and professional settings.

Research

Heathfield (2020), who has been in management and company ownership for more than thirty years, states that "integrity is the foundation on which coworkers build relationships and trust, and it is one of the fundamental values that employers seek in the employees that they hire." She adds that employers and employees with integrity "don't compromise on their ideals, cut corners, cheat, or lie. They behave according to an internally consistent code of values" that lays the groundwork for a successful business (Heathfield, 2020).

According to management executive Cynthia Kincaid (2009), employers expect their employees to make sound ethical decisions regardless of whether employees' positions are entry level or higher ranking within the organization. In fact, businesses tend to communicate this and related employee expectations through their mission and vision statements. Companies also use these statements to convey a specific message to their potential clients or customers—those who will seek them out for equipment, products, or services. In this way, such companies share their moral compass and guiding principles, which outline the integrity and ethical conduct that they promise to reflect in their practices. How businesses conduct themselves and establish their policies and procedures is how they expect their employees—their representatives—to conduct themselves.

Writing for the *Harvard Business Review*, organizational-transformation consultant Ron Ashkenas (2011) explains that in "mission, vision, and value statements . . . almost every company includes a statement about integrity," and he presents information that educators should embrace as they discuss this topic with students. While Ashkenas (2011) agrees that every company should emphasize integrity, he shares two reasons why employees often stumble: (1) the ability to rationalize one's behavior and (2) the range of definitions for *integrity*. To elaborate on the former, he describes an apt situation involving high school students: when asked if cheating is right or wrong, they will say that is it wrong, but if asked whether they have ever cheated—and if given the opportunity to provide examples—they are likely to respond differently (Ashkenas, 2011). What if a friend was sick and missed class, so you let her copy the answers for part of the assigned homework? What if you left your test lying on your desk so your neighbor could compare his answers to yours? Many high school students would not think of these situations as involving cheating. They might talk themselves out of thinking they had done anything wrong at all—thus, the ability to rationalize. It's essential to explore this with students so that they may work against this inclination and think more seriously about ethics, values, and integrity.

Australia's Core Skills for Work framework identifies the "capacity to recognize and respond to differing values, beliefs and behaviors, to draw on diverse perspectives for work purposes and to manage conflict when it arises" as key training needed to bridge the skill gap in the workforce (Australian Government, n.d.). Consider again the example of the career center student who requested to end his internship with the auto-services dealership. The ability to challenge the status quo takes time to develop, but teammates hold this characteristic in high regard (Australian Government, n.d.). Training students to understand and embody certain values and ethics is key to the successful management of workplace proceedings, just as in the classroom. As a teacher, you need to help your students both learn and practice ethical strategies as they transition into adulthood and enter careers.

Talking to students about how they carry themselves and the actions that speak to who they are and who they want to become has been part of our mentoring process in education and other professions. Teachers, mentors, and coaches play a key role in setting these high expectations and helping students develop character and tenacity—solid preparation for lives and careers built on high moral standards.

Relay

You can use a variety of instructional methods to help students understand ethics, values, and integrity and how they link to interpersonal relationships and work-related situations. You don't have to limit yourself to typical classroom lectures, as engaging, creative activities for ensuring students' comprehension and enjoyable, practical learning are within your reach. This chapter's skill set affords instructors opportunities to open up thoughtful discussions, design reflection-based writing activities, and assist with students' personal character assessment as they participate in authentic experiences. Students can develop and really hone their ethical decision-making skills through the practice of real-life scenarios. Understanding what they value personally as well as professionally may initially be difficult for students, as their tendency may be to consider what they value in terms of money or possessions, so be prepared to provide guidance as needed.

WHAT'S IN YOUR CARDS?

This activity, which we adapted from William R. Miller, Janet C'de Baca, Daniel B. Matthews, and Paula Wilbourne (2011) of the University of New Mexico, challenges students to think more deeply about values. Students, either individually or in groups, will work through a set of index cards featuring words that they must categorize as important in the work environment and on a personal level. Different individuals and different groups will likely choose very different words, yet common themes tend to arise and make for lively conversation. Note that each card may include either just a word or a word and its definition; just make sure all levels of learners can participate fully.

Materials

For this activity, you will need to assemble the following.

- 1 set of index cards featuring ethics- and value-related words, with or without definitions, per group or individual student (see figure 7.1, page 94)

Individuality	Compassion
Freedom	Dedication
Creativity	Accountability
Wisdom	Knowledge
Humor	Collaboration
Trustworthiness	Helpfulness
Loyalty	Money
Security	Recognition

Figure 7.1: Ethics and values cards.

*Visit **go.SolutionTree.com/21stcenturyskills** for a free reproducible version of this figure.*

Directions for Groups

To carry out the activity with students, follow these steps.

1. Pass out a set of index cards (figure 7.1) to each group of three to five students; every group should be seated at a separate large table that has been cleared of books and other personal belongings.

2. Ask the students to lay all the cards out faceup so they can see each card.

3. Have group members work together to determine the top five words that represent their values and ethics. Give them ten to fifteen minutes to read and discuss the cards and make their decision. Some groups may be able to identify their values quickly, while others will need a bit more time. Be patient and allow plenty of time for every group to select its five values. Also, if you are using sets of cards featuring definitions, inform students that the connotations are somewhat subjective and the students do not have to agree with or accept the precise definitions you've recorded.

4. Instruct groups to leave those five cards faceup and place the remaining cards facedown in a stack.

5. Have each group report out, and record everyone's answers on a whiteboard, tallying up how many times each value is cited.

6. Ask the groups why they selected certain words. Identify which words repeated across multiple groups, and check whether any appeared on all lists. Ask students to discuss differences between their lists, as well as surprises.

7. Repeat steps 2 through 6, but this time with the group selecting the values that its members would want in the companies they hope to work for. The discussion here focuses on what the company would need to value to make it attractive to prospective employees, but it will also be necessary to hark back to groups' previously chosen personal values.

Directions for Individuals

To carry out the activity with students, follow these steps.

1. Pass out a set of index cards to each student.

2. Ask the students to clear their desks and lay the cards out faceup so they can see each card.

3. Ask the students to study the cards for five to ten minutes and identify the words they personally hold as important. If you are using sets of cards featuring definitions, inform students that the connotations are somewhat subjective and the students do not have to agree with or accept the precise definitions you've recorded. Some students may be able to identify their values quickly, while other students will need a bit more time. Be patient, and allow plenty of time for everyone to select five cards.

4. Instruct students to leave those five cards faceup and place the remaining cards facedown in a stack.

5. Ask students whether they would feel comfortable allowing others to see the values that they have chosen. If they are, record everyone's answers on a whiteboard, tallying up how many times each value is cited. Allow students to pass on this step of the activity if they do not feel comfortable sharing in front of others. Invite students to discuss any surprises about the number of times a particular value is shared, and ask students why they chose particular values.

6. Repeat steps 2 through 5, but this time with students selecting the values that they would want in the companies they hope to work for. The discussion here focuses on what the company would need to value to make it attractive to prospective employees, but it will also be necessary to hark back to students' previously chosen personal values.

Homestretch

This activity engages students in self-reflection as they work to decide on the core values that resonate with their moral compass. Understanding the way people conduct themselves in personal and professional settings allows for comprehensive discussions around the values we hold as important and those we wish to see in employers—values that may or may not always overlap. Teachers in comprehensive high schools have reported that use of this activity in a seminar-style discussion has enhanced interactions among students, specifically students who normally struggle to express themselves verbally, as they're able to make use of the cards featuring definitions. Additionally, this activity can spark new ideas among teachers and students and help them view classroom content or previous units in a new light. Facilitating such thoughtful and all-inclusive conversations leads to students' developing a keener sense of good and bad, or right and wrong, and a greater appreciation of ethics and values.

WORKPLACE-ETHICS CASE STUDIES

In this activity, students review realistic workplace scenarios in small groups, make decisions about them, and then share out their ideas with the whole class. For students who are capable of in-depth discussion, scenarios such as those in figure 7.2 work very well. However, sometimes, it is better to initiate discussion about ethical decisions using a more-structured format or simpler dialogue, so make considerations based on grade level. For example, if you are working with a group of young students, you may choose to create a chart, either paper or digital, in which students can jot down their responses as a starting point, rather than simply having an open discussion.

Materials

For this activity, each student group will need the following.

- 1 printed-out set of workplace-ethics case studies (such as those in figure 7.2)

Directions

To carry out the activity with students, follow these steps.

1. Divide the class into small groups of four to five students, and provide each group with a set of case studies.

2. Have group members read through the scenarios and discuss what they think the person in each scenario should do.

3. Have groups share out their case-study solutions with the class, and facilitate deeper class discussions. Discussions should involve students breaking down each scenario into different key components and exploring the *whys* and *hows* of each dilemma.

Case Study 1

Mary is an administrative assistant in the human-resources department. Her good friend Michael is applying for a job with the company, and she has agreed to be a reference for him. Michael asks her for advice on preparing for the interview. Mary has access to the interview questions asked of all applicants and considers making Michael a copy of the list so he can prepare.

Case Study 2

Bob works in the quality-control department. Once a year, his supervisor gives away the company's used computers to the local elementary school. The company does not keep records of these computer donations. Bob really needs a computer at home. His supervisor has asked him to deliver twelve computers to the school.

Case Study 3

Jim is an assistant in the building-services department. He has just received a new work computer and is excited to try it out. Jim wants to learn the email software. His supervisor has a strict policy about computer usage being for business purposes only, but Jim figures one good way to learn this software is to send emails to his friends and relatives until he gets the hang of it. He has finished all his work for the day and has thirty minutes left until his shift is over. His supervisor has left work early.

Case Study 4

Sally was recently hired to work as a receptionist for the front lobby. As receptionist, she is responsible for making copies for the people in her office. Her son, Jason, comes in and needs some copies for a school project. He has brought his own paper—enough for the thirty copies he needs for his class. If he doesn't bring the copies with him to school, he will fail the project. The company copier does not require a security key, and the company does not keep track of copies made by departments.

Source: Adapted from Workforce Solutions, n.d.

Figure 7.2: Workplace-ethics case studies.

Homestretch

By taking part in this activity, students will be able to gain self-awareness and self-confidence as they practice making ethically sound decisions. Note, too, that you can adapt this activity, instead disseminating the scenarios to individual students as a jumping-off point for a written-reflection assignment or a persuasive essay in, for example, an English language arts classroom. The concepts of ethics, values, and integrity can and should be integrated into various content areas.

INTEGRITY IN ACTION

This activity allows students to think about integrity by means of watching a music video. The music video that we've used to outline this activity is of country musician

Clay Walker's song "The Chain of Love" (though you may of course choose a different music video or different song lyrics that illustrate values and ethics through storytelling). It depicts what happens when people choose to do something nice for someone because somebody did something nice for them and how positive actions often come full circle. The video opens with a young man helping an older woman by changing her tire. The woman in turn tips a young woman very well at a local diner. At the end of the video, viewers discover that the young woman is in a relationship with the young man from the video's beginning.

Materials

For this activity, you'll need the following.

- An electronic device on which you can play "The Chain of Love" by Clay Walker (or perhaps "Rise Up" by Andra Day or "Hall of Fame" by the Script—any music video or song that tells a story involving making a decision with a set of ethics or values)

- 1 copy of the integrity-in-action learning grid (figure 7.3) per student

- 1 pen or pencil per student

Mastery	Interpersonal
Describe what the artist is singing about in the song.	What is your personal reaction to this music-video story?
Give your own definition of integrity based on this song.	Have you ever been in a situation similar to any of those described in the song?
Understanding	**Self-Expression**
What is the most important message or point of this song?	On the back of this sheet, draw a picture that illustrates what integrity might look like in the workplace.

Figure 7.3: Integrity-in-action learning grid.

*Visit **go.SolutionTree.com/21stcenturyskills** for a free reproducible version of this figure.*

Directions

To carry out the activity with students, follow these steps.

1. Provide each student with a copy of the integrity-in-action learning grid (figure 7.3).

2. For the class, play Clay Walker's "The Chain of Love" or any song that tells a story that involves using one's ethics or values to make a decision.

3. Have students read the questions and prompts in the integrity-in-action learning grid and record their answers.

4. Discuss with students their responses. Have them describe other examples of poetry, movies, or music that illustrate integrity or value-based decision making.

Homestretch

This powerful activity allows learners at all levels to connect in some way to the concepts we set forth in this chapter. Incorporating music into the classroom is an excellent way to ensure that the content resonates with students. For every music genre, there is a song that is applicable to this activity, so you'll be able to mix things up with different classes and stay current.

Conclusion

It's important that you give your students ample opportunities both to reflect on the attributes they hold dear and to think through how they can act ethically and make value-based decisions in challenging scenarios. In this way, you'll increase the likelihood that students will adhere to ethical standards in their chosen careers. The activities in this chapter provide not only classroom teachers but also counselors, advisers, and other youth workers with multiple avenues for working with groups of various sizes. Conversations lead from the intrapersonal to the interpersonal—and how individuals can shift their thinking to apply personal values to future workplace settings. When people's behavior and words remain consistent with their values, they demonstrate potential for success in the workplace. Businesses must be able to trust employees in order to grow a thriving workforce.

CHAPTER 8

Networking and Interview Know-How

As educators, we know there are questions that you just don't ask in an initial interview. There are also certain things that you *should* work into an interview or conversation with a professional—questions, comments, and terms that signal to the other person your level of understanding or interest. We tactfully share this information with students to prepare them for the challenges they will meet when they show up to their first face-to-face interviews. Knowing how to conduct yourself in such professional situations, or knowing what to say and what not to say, absolutely requires a specific set of skills, and students need to hone these skills and learn what an interviewer is looking for with regard to a candidate's answers and level of engagement. The more opportunities a student has to discuss with teachers and classmates what is appropriate to say and do during an interview, the more confident the student will feel when the time comes to meet with a potential employer—and he or she will be in a better position to showcase his or her unique talents and skills and receive a job offer.

Networking opportunities provide a springboard for students to connect with industry professionals and get a feel for what to share and inquire about. Inviting professionals to your school or center will allow students to sit in a comfortable, familiar location, which can ease tension and foster conversation. Employer panels, guest speakers, and practice interview opportunities give students a chance to learn directly from the industry experts and develop a realistic view of the working community. In fact, mock interviews can prove to be real interviews if a particular business needs employees and the representative sees certain students as viable candidates. On more than one occasion at the career center, employers who have interviewed students have asked to keep their résumés or extend job offers based on impressions the students have left.

Preparing students for interviews in traditional and behavioral questioning creates well-rounded interviewees. Traditional questioning is composed of simple questions that revolve around job responsibilities and prompt more generalized responses. Behavioral questioning differs in that candidates respond to queries by touching on the specific skills and experiences they have that connect to the position at hand, as well as process through scenarios to find concrete solutions. Coordinating interviews (to take place on your school's campus) with company representatives means you are breaking down barriers for students, opening doors, and helping build their confidence about their futures. In this chapter, you'll learn more about the *whys* and the *hows* for delivering these types of industry opportunities to your students.

Rationale

Throughout the years, numerous former students visit Hoosier Hills Career Center. They enjoy coming in to share about their career and educational accomplishments after having attended classes in our building. Our focus at Hoosier Hills is on removing barriers and placing students in the best-possible positions for career success, and hearing about that success generates excitement among the staff.

During one such visit, a Hoosier Hills graduate returned to recount his experience in entering a sheet-metal workers' union. This graduate, Scott, walked into the administrative office puffed up with pride and with a wide smile on his face, asking the receptionist whether it would be OK to briefly speak with the director. As he told the director about the interview and training process he had undergone at the sheet-metal workers' union, his confidence became contagious. Because of this, although Scott had planned to speak only with his former welding teacher for a few minutes during the teacher's break, he found himself standing in front of the entire welding-and-machining class.

Scott spoke of his high school classroom experience and the interviews he'd had, which had allowed him to speak directly to the sheet-metal workers' union contacts prior to graduation. He also spoke about the panel interview that he'd had more recently with the union training program. The people on the panel had started with the usual questions and then asked where he'd trained during high school. Scott said that once he mentioned Hoosier Hills Career Center, those on the panel lit up and started sharing the names of other students who had joined the union from the same high school program. The main interviewer then asked Scott to step out so the panel could discuss his application and interview results. When Scott returned to the room, the panel reported that because of his scores, his previous training, and his professionalism in the interview process, he would be placed right into the apprenticeship rather than a two-year preapprenticeship program. That meant he'd start at eighteen dollars an hour rather than the fourteen an hour reserved for preapprentices. What a meaningful achievement for Scott and a testament to his well-rounded abilities.

There is no more perfect rationale for teaching networking and interview skills than the chance to give students training that will impact their very livelihoods. While it's true that technical skills are a significant component of career success, the employability-skills framework and the real-world experiences that accompany it provide students with the ability to talk with others about what they have learned, elaborate on their accomplishments, and share details of the skills they can bring to the career field. They also help students build a solid résumé and truly pave the way for them to realize their employment ambitions.

Research

Various organizations focus on assisting young people through mentorship. Big Brothers Big Sisters, for example, serves school-age youth by facilitating positive relationships with adults, allowing youth to network and make meaningful connections. The organization aims to provide youth with examples of stable relationships, bringing adults and youth together through educational, leisure, and career activities (Social Programs That Work, 2017). This model is successful on a global scale, with school- and community-based partnerships that stretch to serve youth with a wide variety of occupational interests. The same goals of connectedness and future focus are evident in our employability-skills framework. The research here demonstrates the value of using training experiences in which young people learn skills for personal and occupational achievement while being mentored. Networks of leaders who focus on spending time to share about career and educational options for students create a pathway for successful attainment of personal and professional goals.

Dan Hull (2005), principal investigator and executive director of the National Center for Optics and Photonics Education, concludes that goals of education in the 21st century have strayed from helping students become responsible citizens, make career choices, continue with postsecondary education, and set long-term goals. Rather, it has turned into a standardized-test training facility that focuses on a small portion of course content and disregards instruction in the areas of interest to students (Hull, 2005). He describes a need to give students career-pathway guidance and to link all aspects of students' education as they relate to their lives and employment goals (Hull, 2005). Educational consultants Debra Bragg and Debra Mills (as cited in Hull, 2005) collaborate on career-pathway programming to create real partnerships that, when used properly, enhance and ease students' transition from secondary education to postsecondary pursuits. Bragg and Mills focus on a collective approach to meeting students' needs via industry partnerships; this approach includes recommended connections found to improve the desired outcomes for CTE students, including networking sessions, tours of industry, and participation in information panels in which speakers discuss the newest processes or equipment (Hull, 2005). This employability-skills framework provides students with such real-world connections. These connections can come in the form of employer participation in employer panels and one-on-one interview sessions. This gives students experience and ultimately serves both parties, often by translating into future recruitment.

Relay

When you engage with industry partners, it is important that you be clear with them about your needs and expectations. For instance, industries need a future workforce, without a doubt; however, they do not have time for multiple events to recruit from one location. If you want to build positive relationships with your industry partners, you must be mindful of the amount of time they truly have to offer. If you want them to attend a career fair or conduct interviews with students, say so explicitly. Educators often have difficulty asking for precisely what they need from business partners. Keep it clear and simple to start a great relationship, and ask them to attend only one event. Note that various networking events, such as career fairs, hold opportunities for professionals to interact with students around a central set of goals they both share. Speaking with industry partners in their particular fields of interest helps students build strong connections to those careers. These connections are the stepping-stones that students need to transition into adulthood. It is not without planning that networking and interview know-how fall at the end of the employability-skills curriculum at the career center. We carefully manage the learning objectives of each employability skill in such a way as to prepare students for the face-to-face conversations they will have about their future careers. A student's evolution from day one of employability-skills lessons to an interview session is absolutely priceless.

Students in career centers gain an advantage when employers attend their open-house events. Employers have the chance to view students in welding labs or culinary kitchens, where they can show off their skills. Comprehensive schools and career centers alike can host employer panels by starting small and building partnerships. It is essential for students to each prepare a brief elevator pitch about their abilities and career aspirations to share during interviews. Helping students know how to present themselves and ask on-point questions simply creates well-prepared young adults.

SAMPLE QUESTIONS FOR EMPLOYER PANELS

An employer panel is designed to give students the opportunity to learn directly from local employers about company expectations for résumés, interviews, and workplace behavior. Typically, having between five and nine panel members from two or three career fields is more than enough for a successful panel discussion. Lead students in the process of creating a list of appropriate and prioritized questions for the panel.

Materials

For this activity, you'll need the following.

- Blackboard
- Chalk

Directions

To carry out the activity with students, follow these steps.

1. Prior to inviting professionals into the building, begin by explaining to students how they'll need to come up with positive, focused questions to spark a meaningful dialogue during an upcoming panel discussion. Note that the questions should still be somewhat generic, to cover a broad range of topics for the individual employer.

2. Ask students for suggestion question topics, and help them frame the questions in a positive fashion. If you wish, you can present some of the following sample questions to help students start brainstorming.

   a. Do you prefer receiving chronological or functional résumés? Why?

   b. What are the top skills you are looking for in an employee?

   c. Are you willing to conduct mock interviews?

   d. What are some tips that can help us better prepare for our interviews?

   e. What is the biggest negative when it comes to interviewing job applicants?

   f. What is your workplace environment like?

   g. Do you have special rules about using cell phones on the job?

   h. What is the number-one reason you must terminate an employee?

   i. Do you encourage employees to further their educations, or do you provide tuition assistance?

   j. What do you feel is proper dress for an interview?

    k. What type of information should we research about potential employers prior to interviewing with them?

    l. What types of references do you like applicants to provide?

3. Record students' questions on the blackboard.

4. Word process the list, print it, and distribute it so that employers can see the questions in preparation for their panel discussion. Students should also have a copy of the questions for reference during the discussion, as they may get nervous and forget something they wanted to ask.

Homestretch

It is important to ensure that students ask the questions in a positive and respectful manner. In most panel discussions we have witnessed, students conduct themselves appropriately. At the career center, students truly listen and take in the information that these industry personnel share. They pay attention and take time to look up information about the companies they are interested in interviewing with and working for. Students use the span of time between the panel session and the interview day to hone their skills and make last-minute adjustments to their résumés. This same experience can be replicated in a comprehensive school.

It is common to have college representatives visit high schools for an evening. What if you also offered interview time with regional employers during such an event? Giving students a chance to interview with potential employers in a comfortable environment could result in their landing a summer internship or a job, postsecondary training, or postsecondary education following high school graduation. Once students realize that adults are listening to them and giving them perspectives that will assist them in securing positions with these companies, they are grateful and even more motivated.

INTERVIEW QUESTIONS

An interview practice that is becoming more popular with companies involves behavioral interview questions. In traditional interviews, job applicants typically answer questions that require little more than *yes* or *no* responses or questions that invite them to talk about their skills. They also respond to questions regarding what they might be doing in five years. Behavioral interview questions, though, prompt applicants to give scenario-based examples. A question such as "When was a time you showed that you could be a leader?" calls for a response vastly different from what applicants would give to a traditional interview question. Students need practice answering both types of questions but may need more practice with behavioral questions so they can form clear examples from their previous experiences. It takes time and requires much thought to prepare compelling, relevant examples, so students should practice with a teacher or mentor to better understand the desired responses.

Materials

For this activity, you'll need the following.

- 1 word-processed list of possible interview prompts and questions (see figure 8.1) per student

- 1 pen or pencil per student

- Tell me a little about yourself.

- Tell me why you are interested in this position.

- What three words would you use to describe yourself?

- What do you think are the most important abilities that lead to success on the job?

- Give an example of a time when you had to be strategic to meet all tasks you were assigned.

- How do you think a supervisor would describe your work ethic?

- Tell me about a time when you made a mistake and how you were able to rectify the situation.

- Give me an example of a time when you handled a stressful situation in the workplace particularly well.

Figure 8.1: Interview prompts and questions.

Visit go.SolutionTree.com/21stcenturyskills for a free reproducible version of this figure.

Directions

To carry out the activity with students, follow these steps.

1. Pass out a sheet of interview prompts and questions to students. Ask students to read and carefully consider each item before taking the time to record their answers.

2. Once you've allowed students to write down their answers, instruct students to get into pairs and take turns asking and answering the questions. Explain that they should not memorize answers to these questions verbatim but rather use these questions and written responses as a general guide, to help them better express their thoughts and experiences.

Homestretch

Students need to know that it is important to always be honest when answering questions during an interview. You will also need to explain that they should try to be diplomatic in their responses. Politically charged answers can backfire, and being too carefree or lighthearted can be viewed negatively. Remind students to stay calm and respond only to the question posed, rather than continuing on for too long—though the longer, more thoughtful responses should follow the behavioral types of questions that often begin with the phrase "Give me an example." Reiterate to students that if they remain positive and as natural as possible, the interview will seem more like a conversation than an interrogation—but it takes practice to learn the art of the interview process.

Conclusion

During the networking and interview processes, students realize that the professional adults involved have come to genuinely help them make informed decisions about their futures. Industry partners sincerely engage with the students, sharing personal and professional perspectives on students' career interests. It is an incredible process. During use of the employability-skills framework, buy-in develops with the students and leads to strong connections for the students with their teachers, mentors, and even the potential employers. And the students often truly impress the industry partners. In a conversation we had with local fire-department personnel after career-center students interviewed with them, they told us that the students nailed their interviews and had the interviewers wondering whether the students had received their exact questions beforehand. The students were so articulate during the behavioral interview process that they shocked the interviewers. What a testament to the fact that giving students interviewing and networking opportunities creates strong communication skills and self-confidence.

CHAPTER 9

Career-Pathway Preparation

Career-pathway preparation assists students in identifying career interests through exploring and setting a relevant course of action in an educational program of study. According to Advance CTE (n.d.), in the United States, career pathways are multiyear programs established from the sixteen national career clusters of (1) agriculture, food, and natural resources; (2) architecture and construction; (3) arts, audiovisual technology, and communications; (4) business management and administration; (5) education and training; (6) finance; (7) government and public administration; (8) health sciences; (9) hospitality and tourism; (10) human services; (11) information technology; (12) law, public safety, corrections, and security; (13) manufacturing; (14) marketing; (15) science, technology, engineering, and mathematics; and (16) transportation, distribution, and logistics. Each U.S. state is responsible for approving a list of career pathways, and individual school districts then select the pathways most suited to their areas. Each career pathway charts a journey through the program of study, sequence of courses, and recommended activities, such as job shadowing and work-based learning experiences, to provide students with marketable skills and lay the foundation for postsecondary options. Helping students navigate career-pathway preparation is the most basic and necessary step in the employability-skills framework. "So why not place this chapter at the beginning of the book?" you might ask. Truly, this chapter demands the most work from stakeholders—that is, students, parents, counselors, faculty advisers, teachers, and potentially the career-pathway businesses involved. Figuring out future plans as a young person can be daunting and overwhelming, and students often research specific careers of interest, in addition to completing self-assessments and personal inventories that indicate aptitude and interest. Researching with students, connecting with students, and spending one-on-one time with students takes teachers' dedication and time. Parents and guardians, too, play a key role in assisting students with career-pathway and course-selection decisions. This takes logistical talent, follow-through, and follow-up. It takes precious time. And it's all well worth the effort in the end.

In previous chapters, it was important that we share how readily teachers can integrate an activity or how they can use a few rationale points to really drive home the importance of a targeted employability skill. Every preceding skills chapter provided research-based content and activities for instruction across the curriculum with regard to college and career readiness. This chapter lays the foundation for students to discover a career interest and select a career pathway, and it helps students start to think about the more technical knowledge, skills, and abilities they need for the careers they seek, as well as educational requirements and anticipated wages. After we explore the rationale and research behind career-pathway preparation, the activities in this chapter will help students work toward this career fulfillment through self-awareness of their aptitudes, personality traits, and interests.

Rationale

Career-pathway preparation plays a significant role in preparing all students for their futures. For students to make better decisions, they must familiarize themselves with possibilities and the job market by studying a variety of career opportunities. Career pathways provide awareness, exploration, and preparation, giving more relevancy to students' learning.

Through our work, we have found work-based learning to be extremely beneficial for students to prepare for a career and learn more about the day-to-day responsibilities of a given occupation. We have found job shadowing, industry tours, guest speakers, employer panels, internships, cooperative education, and apprenticeships to be valuable components in the learning process, allowing for a realistic and more in-depth study of a career. Aside from gaining an understanding of what to discuss in a professional context, students who have the chance to hear professionals share their firsthand experience will be empowered to work toward their own professional goals.

Key components of a work-based learning experience, which usually occurs during senior year, include a thoughtful connection of a student to an employer, the application process, safety and liability considerations, and a training agreement. Setting up an avenue for students to apply and having specific criteria in place are essential in a quality work-based learning program. Criteria might include good attendance, reliable transportation, and enrollment in courses relevant to the industry. Note that before sending any student out of the building, you must receive approval from the administration, and administrators may need to seek additional information from the school attorney or insurance company regarding the issue of liability. Training agreements outline and clarify supervision, learning objectives, and evaluation plans, explaining what all involved parties, including the student, parents, school, and employer, are responsible for in the partnership. We recommend a school have a central point of contact for the businesses—that is, not every teacher should be working independently with businesses.

Reflecting on a fruitful work-based learning experience, we thought of a student who'd been in an internship class at a comprehensive high school. Carla was a senior and planning on a career in sports medicine. When she requested an internship, she was placed in the office of a prominent physician who specialized in sports injuries. During the semester, Carla was able to spend more than seventy hours in the medical office, and she worked alongside the doctor's lead nurse. At the conclusion of the course, Carla made her final presentation and said she had decided to change her career focus. She had witnessed the interaction among nurses and patients and realized that, although the doctor was indeed in the patients' rooms taking notes and checking in after procedures, the nurses were the ones who performed the hands-on application of wraps and splints and administered other treatments. She determined that patient contact seemed most rewarding and appealing, so she switched her career pathway. Some might be tempted to view this as a failure, in that Carla did not follow what she'd originally set out to do—but that's far from the truth. The personal growth and realizations that took place during the internship allowed this student to determine the best plan for herself and her life. In Carla's case, the internship course gave her experience in a field before she had to decide on a career pathway. Carla graduated high school and went on to attend a state university, where she obtained a bachelor of science in nursing.

All work-based learning experiences provide an opportunity to target exploration in specific career pathways. Senior-year internships are the most popular work-based learning, allowing for on-the-job training and authentic learning. As ESSA and Perkins V continue to offer guidelines for college and career readiness, it is imperative that teachers connect students directly to experiences that expose them to available career-pathway opportunities so they can make sound decisions for themselves.

Research

According to the Perkins Collaborative Resource Network (n.d.), since the 1990s career clusters and career pathways have evolved with the goal of assisting youth and adults in gaining skills and industry-recognized credentials through the alignment of education, training, and services. Katherine Ruffing (n.d.) of the University of Illinois at Urbana-Champaign writes that initiatives such as Tech Prep, SCANS, and School-to-Work, along with the shift from vocational education to career and technical education, have led to the integration of academic standards and specialty-level technical skills to better prepare students for future careers.

As we look back on philosophies of education, we can support the concept of learning through career pathways and work-based learning experiences. In 1934, John Dewey shared his theory that learners can gain more-concrete understanding through having hands-on educational experiences than through simply reading a text or having a discussion (Stanford Encyclopedia of Philosophy, 2018). Dewey theorized that instruction should focus on the learner's outlook, attitude, and skill development. He initiated a conversation on the progressive educational system that entailed teaching the whole child, emphasizing student ownership in learning rather than rote memory, thus supporting educational developments in inquiry-based instruction and the use of guided questions as a means to explore and engage.

In *Career Planning and Building*, Harry Newton Clarke (1934) shares his philosophy on the importance of personal-interest inventories. Clarke (1934) advocates affording people the opportunity to review the complete mass of information on any field of work they wish to consider. Answering their questions and validating their beliefs and abilities through a personal-interest inventory helps people determine their true career interests and aptitudes. In this way, individuals can make clearly informed life-work choices (Clarke, 1934).

Research has shown that different personality types tend to correspond with certain career preferences. In developing the Myers–Briggs Type Indicator, Katharine Cook Briggs and Isabel Briggs Myers focused their work on self-indication and self-reflection around personal aptitudes, and Briggs worked twenty years testing and validating the questions used for the instrument. Published in 1962, the Myers–Briggs Type Indicator is the most used personality indicator instrument in the world to match applicants to jobs and enhance workplace communication (Myers-Briggs Company, n.d.). According to Isabel Briggs Myers, Mary H. McCaulley, Naomi L. Quenk, and Allen L. Hammer (1998), multiple industries use the Myers–Briggs Type Indicator to assist with employment decisions around interests and abilities typical for success in their fields. Psychologists Gary D. Gottfredson and John L. Holland (1996) also researched and revolutionized the interest-inventory connection to the types of careers that satisfy individuals' needs through alignment of work values and abilities.

Relay

Providing students with opportunities to identify personality traits, aptitudes, and interests will be beneficial as students determine career possibilities. Educators must help students realize that once they can pinpoint what they enjoy and what they need for personal fulfillment, they can find their best-fit careers. Better understanding their personality traits, too, will aid students in selecting a career pathway in which they are most likely to succeed and find their work rewarding and meaningful. In the following activities, we offer a simple personality assessment inventory, which includes questions to guide career research, and information regarding student job shadowing.

DISCOVERING PERSONALITY TRAITS

This activity allows students to begin to identify the topic areas they find exciting to explore, as well as their personal strengths and weaknesses. Explain to students that the more they understand about their own personalities, the more likely they are to select careers that are rewarding and allow for success.

Materials

Each student will need the following for this activity.

- 1 electronic device with which to access the internet (for example, a personal computer or smartphone)
- 1 copy of the career-interest questionnaire (figure 9.1, page 115)
- 1 pen or pencil

Directions

To carry out the activity with students, follow these steps.

1. Instruct students to use their electronic device to navigate to the My Next Move website (www.mynextmove.org) and select the Start button at the bottom of the box that reads "Tell us what you like to do."

2. Tell students to read the instructions and answer the sixty questions, using the Next button to advance from one screen to the next.

3. Have students review their results and see whether they can identify the personality types that the following questions describe.

   - What personality type likes to work with forms, designs, and patterns? (artistic)
   - What personality type prefers teaching, helping, and healing others? (social)
   - What personality type is usually involved in starting a business or keeping it running? (enterprising)
   - What personality type prefers practical, hands-on problems and solutions? (realistic)

- What personality type likes work that is precise and detail oriented? (conventional)

- What personality type prefers work with critical thinking and abstract ideas? (investigative)

4. Invite students to use the My Next Move website or other locations to find careers of interest that directly reflect their identified personality traits.

5. Tell students to use the career-interest questionnaire (figure 9.1) to identify careers and classes that may help them make a final decision about their best-fit profession. Students should list their top career interests and use the questionnaire to guide course selection and training needed for success in the field of interest. The questionnaire also has a set of questions to assist them with reflecting on their personality type.

Homestretch

This activity provides a framework for classwork that intentionally engages students in the areas of study or career options that interest them. When students understand their areas of interest, they are able to identify the topic areas that will likely make them feel fulfilled and have success in their career. There is a genuine connection between one's traits and one's ultimate career success.

STUDENT JOB SHADOWING

In the south central region of Indiana, several companies have extended offers for our students to shadow employees in various positions. As a result, we have created some easy-to-use forms with which to set up and carry out shadowing opportunities, as well as forms that clearly detail expectations for all involved in the shadowing process. You might ask, "Who should set up the job-shadowing experience if these partnerships have not already been established?" As recommended previously, we believe the school should have a central point of contact for businesses; however, for a job-shadowing experience of no more than a day, the student might reach out to the prospective company and set up the experience, with permission from the school and a parent or guardian. The school should set criteria before allowing job shadowing, and school personnel should oversee the shadowing experience, including paperwork, attendance, and student follow-through. The following activity outlines the necessary steps and forms for successful outreach to companies at which students will shadow employees. Note that for each form, we give suggestions on content, but you will

Top interest level: _____% Career category: _____

Recommended student classes: _____

Example careers: _____

Second interest level: _____% Career category: _____

Recommended student classes: _____

Example careers: _____

Record the basic characteristics of your personality type.

_____

Identify five strengths of your personality.

1. _____

2. _____

3. _____

4. _____

5. _____

Identify five weaknesses of your personality.

1. _____

2. _____

3. _____

4. _____

5. _____

What career pathways would most likely offer satisfaction to you?

_____

What workplace habits might you exhibit?

_____

Make a concluding statement about your personality type.

_____

Figure 9.1: Career-interest questionnaire.

*Visit **go.SolutionTree.com/21stcenturyskills** for a free reproducible version of this figure.*

need to follow your state and school policies, and administration should approve all forms before distribution.

Materials

Each student will need the following for this activity.

- 1 copy of forms A–E

Directions

To carry out the activity with students, follow these steps.

1. Distribute forms A–E to the students. Students who request shadowing experiences should meet criteria guidelines the school has established. Follow the procedures that are most commonly used, such as requiring parent signatures. You may consider creating electronic forms that can be signed and resubmitted via email. School personnel will be responsible for approving the student's request and placement site and collecting all paperwork.

   • **Form A:** Permission to Participate Parent Signature Form

   This is a permission form allowing the student to shadow someone. It should be filled out after the student has secured a business site. General information to include would be the student's name, school name, school contact person, and purpose of the job-shadowing experience. The company's name, contact person, and contact information should be also included on the form. Along with a place for the parent's name, signature, and contact information, note the arranged date, time, and transportation details. In most cases, the student gives this form to a parent or guardian to complete and sign, and the student returns the form to the school personnel in charge of the shadowing.

   • **Form B:** Business and Education Partnership Form

   The company contact person listed on form A receives this informational form. The form gives the business the objectives and desired outcomes of the job-shadowing experience. This form is generally sent with form C as an employer packet. See figure 9.2 (page 118) for an example of this form.

   • **Form C:** Employer Confirmation Form

   This form is important because it confirms the employer's intent to host the student, who will be allowed to shadow someone, on a certain day and time. The form is given to the business, along with form B, to sign and return to the school personnel prior to the shadowing experience. Suggested information to include on the form is business name, contact person, address, direction to worksite, date, time, lunch arrangement, and any special notes, such as an age requirement or general dress code.

- **Form D:** Field Trip Permission Form

    In our school corporation, the field-trip form must be completed and signed by each of the student's teachers at least three days prior to the day of job shadowing and then given to the school personnel in charge of shadowing. A parent or guardian signature is also required on this form.

- **Form E:** Questions to Ask the Business Host

    The student will complete this form during the day of the shadowing, and the student must secure a signature from the business before returning the form to the school contact. Suggested questions might involve company mission, products or services, the department's responsibilities, the employee's responsibility, education requirements, and high school courses recommended for the career.

2. Note to students that forms A, C, and D must be completed and returned to the school personnel before job shadowing can take place. Failure to complete all forms as outlined will result in denial of the shadowing experience.

Homestretch

Job shadowing is an opportunity for students to see what a typical day would be like in a given career. It may inspire a student to learn more and pursue the career, or it may show him or her that it's not a good fit. Both scenarios are a win. Eliminating what you don't want to do is a positive step in discovering what you *do* want to do. Job shadowing is an excellent way to begin career exploration, especially for freshmen. For seniors, we highly recommend internships, cooperative education, and apprenticeships.

Conclusion

Work-based learning gives students access to knowledge and experience that move beyond the classroom setting, even for career and technical education environments. Work-based learning connects students to the real world and allows them to work side by side with professionals. Students gain insight into career targets that go beyond their original thoughts, and it proves to be extremely advantageous to entering the field after high school. With work-based learning, students practice employability skills and

A Business and Education Partnership

Thank you for volunteering your valuable time and allowing our student at [insert school name] the opportunity to shadow you at your place of work. Shadowing experiences allow students to test their career goals in real work settings, and they lead to a more enriched career-pathway program of study.

Objectives for the Job-Shadowing Experience

- To provide realistic work experience in a career field
- To provide occupational and career information
- To develop leadership skills necessary in a career area
- To introduce students to dedicated professionals in the field
- To clarify skills and preparation necessary to a particular field
- To give students knowledge that will assist them in the career decision-making process
- To meet the achievement standards set by [insert state or province]

Desired Outcomes of Job Shadowing

- To introduce students to the skills needed for employment in a community business
- To utilize community resources in the education program
- To involve the community resources in the education program
- To make the education program comprehensive

The student will arrive by way of parent-arranged transportation. The student will plan on being responsible for his or her own lunch unless other arrangements have been made.

If school is closed or delayed because of inclement weather, power failures, or any other reason, all job shadowing will be canceled for that day.

The Employer Confirmation Form (form C) must be returned to the student's instructor prior to the shadowing experience. If the student is not able to return this to the instructor, then it may be mailed to [teacher's name], [school], [street], [city], [state] [zip code], or faxed to [number].

Figure 9.2: Example form B.

*Visit **go.SolutionTree.com/21stcenturyskills** for a free reproducible version of this figure.*

network and communicate with adults, which may lead to a job offer after secondary school or college. This type of learning allows for reflection—and it opens doors. Pairing students with local or regional businesses provides a pipeline of employment options that directly connect to technical-skill training centers at the high school and postsecondary level. Giving your students—potential employees—multiple chances for career preparation makes for long-term employment and sustained interest and engagement, which benefits your students and their eventual employers.

Epilogue

As an educator, you hope that students can take the core of what they learn and use it in some way to find success. Employability skills are key to ensuring your students have what they need as they transition into adult responsibilities. Embedding a comprehensive set of employability skills into your established curriculum will prepare your students to successfully follow through with whatever postsecondary, military, workforce, or apprenticeship plans they choose. As practitioners, we want to offer *all* students college and career readiness. And implementing the core skills from our framework provides students with foundational skills that we have vetted through state, national, and international research data on business and industry, as well as our personal connections with Indiana employers.

In addition to providing college and career readiness, the activities featured in this book support students' social and emotional learning and promote engagement as students develop and hone the essential core skills. It's because of the comprehensive nature of the framework that you should include employability skills in your school's strategic plan, not just as a discussion topic within a career class, a work-based learning course, or CTE programs. Employability skills can easily be integrated into standards across the general curriculum. What subjects in your school are relevant to students' futures? *All of them*—and that is why not only teaching employability skills but tying them to your subject matter heightens relevance.

You or fellow staff may think, "I don't have time to do more," "It's hard to get through what I'm already doing," or "I can't add any more to my curriculum," and as educators, we understand those thoughts. This is why the employability-skills framework is not an add-on; we designed it to intertwine with established lessons, authentic conversations and instruction on career expectations, skill requirements, and ways to navigate the workplace.

Practically speaking, you must make student engagement a key component of your teaching while providing thorough career preparation with a common language around workforce readiness. When students are actively engaged, you'll discover that more learning takes place and fewer discipline issues occur. Activities in our framework allow for this high-level engagement and lead to students' deeper understanding and demonstration of the targeted skills. In your teaching, strive for engagement, encourage collaboration with peers, and reduce the number of problems that have only one right answer. By doing so, you strengthen communication, teamwork, and critical-thinking skills. Utilizing student engagement as a teaching strategy for employability skills, you will quickly see a best practice evolve, providing a space for students to take risks without fear of failure, a place where they are connected. During instruction, you will see an exciting shift take place in students as they build growth mindsets; acknowledge their own strengths and potential, as well as their peers'; and improve their intrapersonal and interpersonal skills—skills crucial for students' successful transition into adult life and the workforce.

The real-life anecdotes we've shared throughout the book illustrate the inextricable link between education and industry. To stop or stall the brain drain in communities and retain the talent necessary to ensure economic stability for the long term, both sides must work together toward like goals. For states and provinces to attract new business and industry, they must have a workforce with clear technical *and* employability skills that meet employer needs. We want to help you equip students with as many tools as possible so they become their best selves and excel throughout their lives. Our framework supports academic standards, recognizes workforce needs, and integrates hands-on learning techniques while acknowledging and teaching mutual respect for individual differences. It provides an avenue for you to meet ESSA regulations, Perkins V for CTE, and additional state laws and mandates. And as you meet these requirements and encourage the development of skills that businesses deem important for workplace success, you will be preparing all students for their futures.

If you are a classroom teacher, incorporate some of the activities in this book, and see an increase in student engagement. You'll also see peer relationships change, as students will embrace mutual respect, demonstrate greater acceptance of others, and more eagerly interact with those outside their usual circle of friends. After students graduate, you will love hearing their success stories that link back to the time they spent in your classroom. This warms our hearts *every single time*. Work to build collaboration and boost face-to-face communication among students. Encourage different approaches and answers to problems and situations. In 21st century education, in which test taking reigns, teachers often communicate to their students that there is only one right answer. But teachers must intentionally highlight the very process of solving problems, of being able to consider and evaluate multiple options; this proves more useful in life and in the workplace. Students' lives are composed of choices, and developing critical-thinking skills is of utmost importance in this constantly changing world in which they live.

In addition to incorporating activities and nurturing employability skills, discover local needs by talking to regional businesses about new hires' strengths and weaknesses. Which skills do the new employees have, and which do they lack? Also, consider the initiatives your state or province has implemented on employability skills. What workforce development resources are in place, and what is at the forefront in education? Educational leaders in your school should investigate what faculty members are doing and how employability skills can be expanded and incorporated into all subjects. Will there be resistance? Yes. There will always be staff who wish for things to remain the same, as that route is safe and easy. But many teachers are agents of change and are willing to give something new a shot if it means making a positive difference in their students' lives.

Your responsibility to students lies in providing the best instruction and education in the development of academic, technical, and employability skills. Using the employability-skills framework will launch you forward in connecting business needs and educational preparation and will prove invaluable to students and their futures. Leading students through intentional instruction toward careers that intrigue, challenge, satisfy, and provide fulfillment is accomplished through authentic student learning. When you take a minute to reflect on the impact you have had on your students' lives, we trust you will see a return on your investment in using our employability-skills framework.

Appendix

Ready for the Workforce evolved from the employability-skills curriculum we developed in 2016. To align and validate the curriculum, we created a crosswalk of Indiana Department of Education academic standards for various subjects; Indiana's Department of Workforce Development Employability Skills Benchmarks; the U.S. Department of Education Office of Career, Technical and Adult Education employability-skills framework; the Commonwealth of Australia Core Skills for Work Developmental Framework; and the Conference Board of Canada employability skills. The purpose of the crosswalk is to show how our framework links subject matter taught in a school setting with the skills employers deem essential, and to provide educators with further rationale for embedding the framework into the classroom to prepare all students for the global workplace.

Table A.1: Crosswalk of Employability Skills and Academic Standards

Youth Employability Skills Framework	Indiana Academic Standards Indiana Department of Education	Indiana Employability-Skills Benchmarks Indiana Department of Workforce Development	Employability Skills Framework U.S. Department of Education Office of Career, Technical, and Adult Education	Core Skills for Work Developmental Framework Australian Government	Employability Skills The Conference Board of Canada
COMMUNICATION	ENGLISH LANGUAGE ARTS JAG COMPETENCIES MATHEMATICS PREPARATION FOR COLLEGE AND CAREERS SOCIAL STUDIES WORK-BASED LEARNING	SOCIAL SKILLS » Oral Communication WORKPLACE SKILLS » Follows Directions	WORKPLACE SKILLS » Communication Skills	INTERACT WITH OTHERS » Communicate for work » Recognize and utilize diverse perspectives	FUNDAMENTAL SKILLS » Communication
TEAMWORK AND COLLABORATION	ENGLISH LANGUAGE ARTS JAG COMPETENCIES MATHEMATICS PREPARATION FOR COLLEGE AND CAREERS WORK-BASED LEARNING	SOCIAL SKILLS » Teamwork	EFFECTIVE RELATIONSHIPS » Interpersonal Skills WORKPLACE SKILLS » Communication Skills	INTERACT WITH OTHERS » Connect and work with others » Communicate for work	TEAMWORK SKILLS » Work with others » Participate in projects and tasks
CRITICAL THINKING AND PROBLEM SOLVING	ENGLISH LANGUAGE ARTS JAG COMPETENCIES MATHEMATICS PREPARATION FOR COLLEGE AND CAREERS WORK-BASED LEARNING	LEARNING STRATEGIES » Problem Solving » Decision Making » Information Gathering	APPLIED KNOWLEDGE » Critical Thinking WORKPLACE SKILLS » Information Use	GET THE WORK DONE » Make decisions » Identify and solve problems	FUNDAMENTAL SKILLS » Think and solve problems

	ENGLISH LANGUAGE ARTS				FUNDAMENTAL SKILLS
GROWTH MINDSET, RESILIENCE, AND GRIT	ENGLISH LANGUAGE ARTS JAG COMPETENCIES PREPARATION FOR COLLEGE AND CAREERS WORK-BASED LEARNING	MINDSETS » Appreciation of Diversity » Intellectual Risk Taking » Self-Confidence SELF-MANAGEMENT » Perseverance	EFFECTIVE RELATIONSHIPS » Interpersonal Skills » Personal Qualities WORKPLACE SKILLS » Communication Skills	INFLUENCING FACTORS » Self-belief and resilience	FUNDAMENTAL SKILLS » Communicate PERSONAL MANAGEMENT SKILLS » Demonstrate positive attitudes and behaviors » Be responsible » Be adaptable
RESOURCE MANAGEMENT	ENGLISH LANGUAGE ARTS JAG COMPETENCIES MATHEMATICS PREPARATION FOR COLLEGE AND CAREERS WORK-BASED LEARNING	LEARNING STRATEGIES » Information Gathering » Organization » Technology Savvy SELF-MANAGEMENT » Professionalism » Stress Management » Time Management SOCIAL SKILLS » Oral Communication » Teamwork WORKPLACE SKILLS » Resource Allocation	EFFECTIVE RELATIONSHIPS » Personal Qualities WORKPLACE SKILLS » Communication Skills » Information Use » Resource Management » Technology Use	GET THE WORK DONE » Plan and organize » Make decisions » Identify and solve problems » Work in a digital world INTERACT WITH OTHERS » Connect and work with others	FUNDAMENTAL SKILLS » Communicate » Think and solve problems PERSONAL MANAGEMENT » Demonstrate positive attitudes and behaviors » Be responsible TEAMWORK » Participate in projects and tasks
WORKPLACE RELATIONSHIP BUILDING	ENGLISH LANGUAGE ARTS JAG COMPETENCIES MATHEMATICS PREPARATION FOR COLLEGE AND CAREERS SOCIAL STUDIES WORK-BASED LEARNING	SELF-MANAGEMENT » Independence » Perseverance » Adaptability	EFFECTIVE RELATIONSHIPS » Personal Qualities » Interpersonal Skills	INTERACT WITH OTHERS » Connect and work with others	FUNDAMENTAL SKILLS » Communicate TEAMWORK » Work with others

continued ▶

ETHICS, VALUES, AND INTEGRITY	ENGLISH LANGUAGE ARTS JAG COMPETENCIES MATHEMATICS PREPARATION FOR COLLEGE AND CAREERS SOCIAL STUDIES WORK-BASED LEARNING	SELF-MANAGEMENT » Integrity » Work Ethic	EFFECTIVE RELATIONSHIPS » Personal Qualities	NAVIGATE THE WORLD OF WORK » Work with roles, rights, and protocols INTERACT WITH OTHERS » Recognize and utilize diverse perspectives INFLUENCING FACTORS » Cultural and value-based factors	PERSONAL MANAGEMENT SKILLS » Demonstrate positive attitudes and behaviors » Work safely
NETWORKING AND INTERVIEW KNOW-HOW	ENGLISH LANGUAGE ARTS JAG COMPETENCIES PREPARATION FOR COLLEGE AND CAREERS SOCIAL STUDIES WORK-BASED LEARNING	LEARNING STRATEGIES » Written Communication » Technology Savvy MINDSETS » Career Path SELF-MANAGEMENT » Professionalism SOCIAL SKILLS » Oral Communication	EFFECTIVE RELATIONSHIPS » Interpersonal Skills WORKPLACE SKILLS » Communication Skills » Information Use » Technology Use	INTERACT WITH OTHERS » Communicate for work » Connect and work with others GET THE WORK DONE » Work in a digital world	FUNDAMENTAL SKILLS » Communicate TEAMWORK SKILLS » Work with others » Participate in projects and tasks
CAREER-PATHWAY PREPARATION	ENGLISH LANGUAGE ARTS JAG COMPETENCIES MATHEMATICS PREPARATION FOR COLLEGE AND CAREERS WORK-BASED LEARNING	LEARNING STRATEGIES » Information Gathering » Problem Solving MINDSET » Career Path SOCIAL SKILLS » Self-Advocacy	APPLIED KNOWLEDGE » Critical Thinking Skills WORKPLACE SKILLS » Information Use » Technology Use	NAVIGATE THE WORLD OF WORK » Manage career and work life GET THE WORK DONE » Make decisions » Work in a digital world	FUNDAMENTAL SKILLS » Manage Information » Think and solve problems PERSONAL MANAGEMENT » Be responsible » Learn continuously

Source: Australian Government, n.d.; Conference Board of Canada, n.d.; Indiana Department of Education, 2020; Indiana Department of Workforce Development; 2019; Office of Career, Technical, and Adult Education, 2015.

References and Resources

Adecco. (2020, February 12). *The American skills gap is real*. Accessed at www.adeccousa.com /employers/resources/skills-gap-in-the-american-workforce/ on December 3, 2020.

Advance CTE. (n.d.). *Career clusters*. Accessed at https://cte.careertech.org/sites/default/files/Career ClustersPathways_0.pdf on November 9, 2020.

American Psychological Association. (2019, November). *Stress in America 2019*. Washington, DC: Author. Accessed at www.apa.org/news/press/releases/stress/2019/stress-america-2019.pdf on January 3, 2020.

American Society for Quality. (n.d.). *Fishbone diagram*. Accessed at https://asq.org/quality-resources /fishbone on December 8, 2019.

Amundson, K. (2019, March). Five questions state boards should ask to advance college and career readiness. *Power of the Question*, *3*(1), 1–4.

Anderson, M., & Jiang, J. (2018, May 31). *Teens, social media and technology 2018*. Washington, DC: Pew Research Center. Accessed at www.pewinternet.org/2018/05/31/teens-social-media -technology-2018 on July 19, 2019.

Ashkenas, R. (2011, February 8). Why integrity is never easy. *Harvard Business Review*. Accessed at https://hbr.org/2011/02/why-integrity-is-never-easy.html on December 8, 2020.

Aspen Institute. (2018, April). *In support of how we learn: A youth call to action*. Washington, DC: Author. Accessed at https://assets.aspeninstitute.org/content/uploads/2018/04/Youth-CTA _FINAL_web.pdf on August 17, 2019.

Association for Career and Technical Education. (2018, February). *CTE: Readiness for all careers*. Accessed at www.acteonline.org/wp-content/uploads/2018/05/ReadinessForAllCareers-FactSheet.pdf on August 5, 2019.

Australian Government. (n.d.). *Core Skills for Work Developmental Framework*. Accessed at www.dese .gov.au/uncategorised/resources/core-skills-work-developmental-framework on December 3, 2020.

Battelle for Kids. (n.d.). *Partnership for 21st Century Learning: A network of Battelle for Kids*. Accessed at www.battelleforkids.org/networks/p21 on August 30, 2019.

Bellis, M. (2019, July 29). *Biography of Cyrus McCormick, inventor of the mechanical reaper*. Accessed at www.thoughtco.com/cyrus-mccormick-mechanical-reaper-1991634 on December 6, 2020.

Berson, A. S., & Stieglitz, R. G. (2013). *Leadership conversations: Challenging high-potential managers to become great leaders*. San Francisco: Jossey-Bass.

Best Schools. (2020, March 23). *The 50 most influential think tanks in the United States*. Accessed at https://thebestschools.org/features/most-influential-think-tanks on July 19, 2019.

Biography. (2019, September 9). *Alexander Graham Bell biography*. Accessed at www.biography.com /inventor/alexander-graham-bell on November 6, 2020.

Biography. (2020, September 24). *Garrett Morgan biography*. Accessed at www.biography.com /inventor/garrett-morgan on November 6, 2020.

Blum, R. W. (2019, May 21). *A global survey sheds new light on how bad events affect young people*. Accessed at https://theconversation.com/a-global-survey-sheds-new-light-on-how-bad-events -affect-young-people-117337 on November 7, 2020.

Bragg, D. D., & Reger, W. M., IV. (2000). Toward a more unified education: Academic and vocational integration in Illinois community colleges. *Journal of Vocational Education Research*, *25*(3), 237–272.

Burton, N. (2012, May 23). Our hierarchy of needs [Blog post]. *Psychology Today*. Accessed at www.psychologytoday.com/us/blog/hide-and-seek/201205/our-hierarchy-needs on September 2, 2019.

C21 Canada. (n.d.). *About us*. Accessed at http://c21canada.org/about-us/ on September 18, 2020.

Center for Teaching Innovation. (n.d.). *Collaborative learning*. Accessed at https://teaching.cornell .edu/teaching-resources/engaging-students/collaborative-learning on October 25, 2020.

Chapman, S. W., & Rupured, M. (2014, April). *Time management: 10 strategies for better time management*. Atlanta: University of Georgia Extension. Accessed at https://extension.uga.edu /publications/detail.html?number=C1042&title=TimeManagement;10StrategiesforBetterTime Management on December 17, 2019.

Clarke, H. N. (1934). *Career planning and building*. Cleveland, OH: Author.

College and Career Readiness and Success Center. (2016, December 13). *Leveraging the employability skills framework for cross-agency collaboration*. Accessed at https://ccrscenter.org/sites/default/files /Leveraging%20Employability%20Skills%20Slides.pdf on November 2, 2020.

Colorado Department of Education. (n.d.). *Career readiness: Essential skills needed for the workforce of educational opportunities beyond high school*. Accessed at www.cde.state.co.us/postsecondary/career readiness on April 27, 2020.

Competency Model Clearinghouse. (n.d.). *Building blocks model*. Accessed at www.careeronestop.org /CompetencyModel/competency-models/building-blocks-model.aspx on August 1, 2019.

Concordia University, St. Paul. (2017, February 10). *Developing effective interpersonal communication skills in the workplace* [Blog post]. Accessed at https://online.csp.edu/blog/business/interpersonal -communication-in-the-workplace/ on December 3, 2020.

Conference Board of Canada. (n.d.). *Employability skills*. Accessed at www.conferenceboard.ca/edu /employability-skills.aspx?AspxAutoDetectCookieSupport=1 on October 27, 2020.

Corporation for National and Community Service. (n.d.). *Eligibility requirements*. Accessed at https://presidentialserviceawards.org/eligibility on January 12, 2020.

Craig, H. (2020, May 19). *Resilience in the workplace: How to be more resilient at work*. Accessed at https://positivepsychology.com/resilience-in-the-workplace on July 14, 2020.

Darling, A. L., & Dannels, D. P. (2003). Practicing engineers talk about the importance of talk: A report on the role of oral communication in the workplace. *Communication Education, 52*(1), 1–16.

DePaoli, J. L., Atwell, M. N., Bridgeland, J. M., & Shriver, T. P. (2018, November). *Respected: Perspectives of youth on high school and social and emotional learning.* Northbrook, IL: Allstate Foundation. Accessed at https://casel.org/wp-content/uploads/2018/11/Respected.pdf on July 11, 2019.

Dewey, J. (1933). *How we think: A restatement of the relation of reflective thinking to the educative process.* Boston: Heath.

Dewey, J. (1938). *Experience and education.* New York: Macmillan.

Duckworth, A. (2016). *Grit: The power of passion and perseverance.* New York: Scribner.

Dweck, C. S. (2014, November). *The power of believing that you can improve* [Video file]. Accessed at www.ted.com/talks/carol_dweck_the_power_of_believing_that_you_can_improve?language=en on July 13, 2020.

Dweck, C. S. (2016). *Mindset: The new psychology of success* (Updated ed.). New York: Random House.

Dweck, C. S., Walton, G. M., & Cohen, G. L. (2014). *Academic tenacity: mindsets and skills that promote long-term learning.* Accessed at https://files.eric.ed.gov/fulltext/ED576649.pdf on November 4, 2020.

Ennis, R. H. (2011, May). *The nature of critical thinking: An outline of critical thinking disposition and abilities.* Accessed at https://education.illinois.edu/docs/default-source/faculty-documents/robert-ennis/thenatureofcriticalthinking_51711_000.pdf on November 26, 2019.

Ethics. (n.d.). In *Merriam-Webster's online dictionary.* Accessed at www.merriam-webster.com/dictionary/ethics on December 8, 2020.

Every Student Succeeds Act of 2015, Pub. L. No. 114-95, 20 U.S.C. § 1177 (2015).

Fica, T. (2019, April 12). *5 ways to help your employees feel valued at work* [Blog post]. Accessed at www.bamboohr.com/blog/employees-feel-valued-at-work/#:~:text=When%20employees%20don%E2%80%99t%20feel%20valued%20at%20work%2C%20it,percent%20higher%20absenteeism%2049%20percent%20more%20workplace%20accidents on November 4, 2020.

Foundation for Critical Thinking. (n.d.). *Defining critical thinking.* Accessed at www.criticalthinking.org/pages/defining-critical-thinking/766 on August 30, 2019.

Garcia, E. (2014, December). *The need to address noncognitive skills in the education policy agenda* (Briefing Paper No. 386). Washington, DC: Economic Policy Institute. Accessed at www.epi.org/publication/the-need-to-address-noncognitive-skills-in-the-education-policy-agenda on February 10, 2020.

Georgia Department of Education. (2016). *Georgia's future workforce.* Accessed at www.gadoe.org/External-Affairs-and-Policy/communications/Documents/Booklet%20EGFW.pdf#search=employability%20skills on April 28, 2020.

Georgia Department of Education. (2019). *CTAE: Partnering with GA's business and industry.* Accessed at www.gadoe.org/Curriculum-Instruction-and-Assessment/CTAE/Documents/CTAE-Annual-Report-2018.pdf#search=international%20skills%20seal on April 27, 2020.

Gottfredson, G. D., & Holland, J. L. (1996). *Dictionary of Holland occupational codes* (3rd ed.). Odessa, FL: Psychological Assessment Resources.

Hart Research Associates. (2013). It takes more than a major: Employer priorities for college learning and student success. *Liberal Education, 99*(2). Accessed at www.aacu.org/publications -research/periodicals/it-takes-more-major-employer-priorities-college-learning-and on June 23, 2020.

Heathfield, S. M. (2020, June 22). *What is integrity?* Accessed at www.thebalancecareers.com/what -is-integrity-really-1917676 on November 5, 2020.

Hewitt, M. (2019, September). Social media: Employability skills for the 21st century. *Techniques: Connecting Education and Careers*, 8–9.

Hulick, K. (2020, September 11). *Healthy screen time is one challenge of distance learning.* Accessed at www.sciencenewsforstudents.org/article/healthy-screen-time-is-one-challenge-of-distance-learning on December 3, 2020.

Hull, D. (2005). *Career pathways: Education with a purpose.* Lanham, MD: Rowman & Littlefield.

Indiana Department of Education. (2020, November 10). *Indiana academic standards.* Accessed at www.doe.in.gov/standards on January 5, 2021.

Indiana Department of Workforce Development. (2019). *Indiana's employability skills benchmarks.* Accessed at www.in.gov/dwd/files/IN_Employability_Skills.pdf on April 29, 2019.

Indiana State University. (n.d.). *Keystone Adventure Program.* Accessed at www.indstate.edu/health /center/soc/kap on November 7, 2020.

International Center for Leadership in Education. (n.d.). *Foundational frameworks.* Accessed at http://leadered.com/our-philosophy/dsei.php on August 18, 2019.

Jensen, E. (2019). *Poor students, rich teaching: Seven high-impact mindsets for students from poverty* (Rev. ed.). Bloomington, IN: Solution Tree Press.

Kelleher, B. (2013, August 20). *Employee engagement: Who's sinking your boat?* [Video file]. Accessed at www.youtube.com/watch?v=y4nwoZ02AJM on October 30, 2019.

Kentucky Department of Education. (2020, May 27). *TRACK: Tech ready apprentices for careers in Kentucky.* Accessed at https://education.ky.gov/CTE/cter/Pages/TRACK.aspx on July 19, 2020.

Kids Count Data Center. (2019). *Children in poverty by age group in the United States.* Accessed at https://datacenter.kidscount.org/data/tables/5650-childreninpovertybyagegroup?loc=1&loc t=1#detailed/1/any/false/37,871,870,573,869,36,868,867,133,38/17,18,36/12263,12264 on January 3, 2020.

Kincaid, C. (2009). Corporate ethics training: The right stuff. *Training, 46*(4), 34–36.

Lagae, K. (2017, October 19). *Henry Ford's 3 recommendations to avoid lousy teamwork.* Accessed at https://medium.com/organize-for-performance/henry-fords-3-teachings-on-successful-teamwork -b44df28b730f on December 4, 2020.

Lang, J. M. (2020, July 15). *With kids spending more waking hours on screens than ever, here's what parents need to worry about.* Accessed at https://theconversation.com/with-kids-spending-more -waking-hours-on-screens-than-ever-heres-what-parents-need-to-worry-about-141261 on January 5, 2021.

Library of Congress & Teaching With Primary Sources. (n.d.). *The Industrial Revolution in the United States*. Accessed at www.loc.gov/teachers/classroommaterials/primarysourcesets/industrial -revolution/pdf/teacher_guide.pdf on November 26, 2019.

Maes, J. D., Weldy, T. G., & Icenogle, M. L. (1997). A managerial perspective: Oral communication competency is most important for business students in the workplace. *Journal of Business Communication, 34*(1), 67–80.

Mann, D. (2018, September). *Welcome to 2018: Get on D.E.C.K.—School counseling updates SY19* [PowerPoint slides]. Accessed at www.gadoe.org/Curriculum-Instruction-and-Assessment/CTAE /Documents/Get-on-DECK-presentation.pdf#search=international%20skills%20seal on April 28, 2020.

Margolis, J. D., & Stoltz, P. G. (2010, January–February). How to bounce back from adversity. *Harvard Business Review, 88*(1–2), 86–92. Accessed at https://hbr.org/2010/01/how-to-bounce -back-from-adversity on January 17, 2020.

Mayo Clinic. (2019, April 4). *Stress symptoms: Effects on your body and behavior.* Accessed at www.mayoclinic.org/healthy-lifestyle/stress-management/in-depth/stress-symptoms/art-20050987 on January 3, 2020.

McDonald, G., Jackson, D., Vickers, M. H., & Wilkes, L. (2016). Surviving workplace adversity: A qualitative study of nurses and midwives and their strategies to increase personal resilience. *Journal of Nursing Management, 24*(1), 123–131. Accessed at www.ncbi.nlm.nih.gov/pubmed/25865519 on February 17, 2020.

McLeod, S. (2020, March 20). *Maslow's hierarchy of needs.* Accessed at www.simplypsychology.org /maslow.html on August 18, 2020.

Miller, W. R., Baca, J. C., Matthews, D. B., & Wilbourne, P. (2011). *Personal values card sort.* Accessed at www.guilford.com/add/miller2/values.pdf?t on October 29, 2020.

Mind Tools. (n.d.a). *5 whys: Getting to the root of a problem quickly.* Accessed at www.mindtools.com /pages/article/newTMC_5W.htm on August 26, 2019.

Mind Tools. (n.d.b). *Forming, storming, norming, and performing: Understanding the stages of team formation.* Accessed at www.mindtools.com/pages/article/newLDR_86.htm on September 2, 2019.

Minnesota Department of Education. (2017, June). *Personal learning plans.* Accessed at https://education.mn.gov/MDE/dse/ccs/plp/index.htm on August 12, 2019.

Minnesota Department of Employment and Economic Development. (2019, September 11). *MN job skills partnership overview* [PowerPoint slides]. Accessed at http://mn.gov/deed/assets/mjsp-overview_tcm1045-403127.pptx on February 8, 2021.

Myers-Briggs Company. (n.d.). *The history of the MBTI® assessment.* Accessed at https://eu.themyers briggs.com/en/tools/MBTI/Myers-Briggs-history on November 11, 2020.

Myers, I. B., McCaulley, M. H., Quenk, N. L., & Hammer, A. L. (1998). *MBTI manual: A guide to the development and use of the Myers–Briggs Type Indicator* (3rd ed.). Palo Alto, CA: Consulting Psychologists Press.

National Association of Colleges and Employers. (2019, March 29). *The four career competencies employers value most.* Accessed at www.naceweb.org/career-readiness/competencies/the-four-career -competencies-employers-value-most on August 30, 2019.

National Institute of Mental Health. (n.d.). *5 things you should know about stress*. Accessed at www.nimh.nih.gov/health/publications/stress/index.shtml on January 6, 2020.

National Network of Business and Industry Associations. (2014). *Common employability skills: A foundation for success in the workplace—The skills all employees need, no matter where they work*. Accessed at https://s3.amazonaws.com/brt.org/archive/Common%20Employability_asingle _fm.pdf on December 8, 2020.

National Science and Technology Council. (2018, December). *Charting a course for success: America's strategy for STEM education*. Washington, DC: White House. Accessed at www.whitehouse.gov /wp-content/uploads/2018/12/STEM-Education-Strategic-Plan-2018.pdf on August 17, 2019.

National Youth Leadership Council. (2008a). *K–12 service learning standards for quality practice*. Accessed at https://cdn.ymaws.com/www.nylc.org/resource/resmgr/resources/lift/standards _document_mar2015up.pdf on August 27, 2020.

National Youth Leadership Council. (2008b). *Standards and indicators for effective service-learning practice*. Accessed at https://cdn.ymaws.com/www.nylc.org/resource/resmgr/k-12_sl_standards _for_qualit.pdf on July 19, 2020.

Nevada Department of Education. (2012, February). *Employability skills for career readiness standards*. Las Vegas, NV: Author. Accessed at www.doe.nv.gov/uploadedFiles/ndedoenvgov/content/CTE /Documents/Employability-Skills-for-Career-Readiness-STDS-ADA.pdf on April 28, 2020.

Ng, B. (2018). The neuroscience of growth mindset and intrinsic motivation. *Brain Sciences, 8*(2), 20. Accessed at www.ncbi.nlm.nih.gov/pmc/articles/PMC5836039 on July 19, 2020.

Office of Career, Technical, and Adult Education. (2015, July 20). *Integrating employability skills: A framework for all educators*. Accessed at https://sites.ed.gov/octae/tag/employability-skills -framework on July 22, 2019.

Office of Career, Technical, and Adult Education. (2016, October 18). *Minority serving community colleges: Uniting for student success*. Accessed at http://conference.novaresearch.com/MSI2016 /agenda.pdf on June 18, 2020.

Office of Population Affairs. (2019, October 3). *The changing face of America's adolescents*. Accessed at www.hhs.gov/ash/oah/facts-and-stats/changing-face-of-americas-adolescents/index.html on December 17, 2019.

Ohio Department of Education. (2017). *Each Child, Our Future: Ohio strategic plan for education— 2019–2024*. Columbus, OH: Author. Accessed at http://education.ohio.gov/About/EachChild OurFuture on April 28, 2020.

Pauley, J. A., & Pauley, J. F. (2009). *Communication: The key to effective leadership*. Milwaukee, WI: ASQ Quality Press.

Payne, R. K. (2019). *A framework for understanding poverty: A cognitive approach* (6th ed.). Highlands, TX: Aha! Process.

Perkins Collaborative Resource Network. (n.d.). *Career pathway systems*. Accessed at https://cte.ed .gov/initiatives/career-pathways-systems on November 9, 2020.

Purdue University. (n.d.). *Lean Six Sigma online*. Accessed at www.purdue.edu/leansixsigmaonline on December 8, 2019.

Radin, J., Hatfield, S., Schwartz, J., & Bordeaux, C. (2020, January 28). *Closing the employability skills gap*. Accessed at https://www2.deloitte.com/us/en/insights/focus/technology-and-the-future -of-work/closing-the-employability-skills-gap.html on November 24, 2020.

Rogacka, O. (2020, June 11). *15 of the best teamwork quotes that will inspire your team to work together*. Accessed at www.livechat.com/success/teamwork-quotes/ on December 4, 2020.

Rosalsky, G. (2020, May 8). *COVID-19 forces more people to work from home. How's it going?* Accessed at www.npr.org/2020/05/08/852527736/covid-19-forces-more-people-to-work-from -home-hows-it-going on November 1, 2020.

Ruffing, K. (n.d.) *The history of career clusters*. Accessed at https://occrl.illinois.edu/docs/libraries provider4/pos/careerclusterhistory.doc on November 11, 2020.

Simpson, D. J., & Stack, S. F., Jr. (Eds.). (2010). *Teachers, leaders, and schools: Essays by John Dewey*. Carbondale, IL: Southern Illinois University Press.

Skillful. (2018, October 11). *Announcing Skillful Indiana*. Accessed at www.skillful.com/indiana on January 4, 2021.

Small Business Sense. (n.d.). *10 famous entrepreneurs that failed in business before becoming successful*. Accessed at https://small-bizsense.com/10-famous-entrepreneurs-who-failed-in-business-before -becoming-successful on January 17, 2020.

Smith, A. P. (2016). Chewing gum and stress reduction. *Journal of Clinical and Translational Research*, *2*(2), 52–54.

Social Programs That Work. (2017, November 20). *Big Brothers Big Sisters*. Accessed at https://evidencebasedprograms.org/programs/big-brothers-big-sisters on October 19, 2019.

Sparks, S. D. (2019, August 7). National study bolsters case for teaching "growth mindset." *Education Week*. Accessed at www.edweek.org/ew/articles/2019/08/07/national-study-shows-how -a-simple-growth.html?cmp=soc-tw-shr on July 19, 2020.

Stanford Encyclopedia of Philosophy. (2018, November 1). *John Dewey*. Accessed at https://plato .stanford.edu/entries/dewey/ on November 11, 2020.

Strengthening Career and Technical Education for the 21st Century Act (Perkins V), Pub. L. 115-224 (2018).

Student Handouts. (n.d.). *Brain teasers and puzzles*. Accessed at www.studenthandouts.com/study -games/printable-games/brain-teasers on January 11, 2020.

Tingum, J. (2019, March 11). How to build effective working relationships. *Houston Chronicle*. Accessed at http://smallbusiness.chron.com/build-effective-working-relationships-20282.html on July 1, 2020.

Truong, L. (2011, August 2). *13 business leaders who failed before they succeeded*. Accessed at www.americanexpress.com/en-us/business/trends-and-insights/articles/13-business-leaders-who -failed-before-they-succeeded on February 17, 2020.

UMass Dartmouth. (n.d.). *Decision-making process*. Accessed at www.umassd.edu/fycm/decision -making/process/ on December 5, 2020.

United States Institute of Peace. (n.d.). *Paper folding activity*. Accessed at http://usip.org/public -education/educators/paper-folding-activity on December 8, 2020.

University of Connecticut. (n.d.). *Critical thinking and other higher-order thinking skills*. Accessed at https://cetl.uconn.edu/critical-thinking-and-other-higher-order-thinking-skills on December 8, 2019.

U.S. Congress. (2018). *Strengthening Career and Technical Education for the 21st Century Act.* Accessed at www.congress.gov/bill/115th-congress/house-bill/2353/text on May 10, 2019.

U.S. Department of Education. (n.d.). *Every Student Succeeds Act.* Accessed at www.ed.gov/essa ?src=rn on August 4, 2019.

U.S. Department of Labor. (n.d.). *Workforce Innovation and Opportunity Act.* Accessed at www.doleta.gov/wioa on August 19, 2019.

U.S. Department of Labor. (1991, June). *What work requires of schools: A SCANS report for America 2000.* Washington, DC: Author. Accessed at https://files.eric.ed.gov/fulltext/ED332054.pdf on July 19, 2020.

U.S. Department of Labor. (2013, April). *Youth in transition.* Accessed at www.dol.gov/odep/topics /youth/softskills on August 10, 2016.

Value. (n.d.). In *Merriam-Webster's online dictionary.* Accessed at www.merriam-webster.com/ dictionary/value on December 8, 2020.

von Zastrow, C. (2018, December 18). *Perkins V: Expanding opportunities for work-based learning* [Blog post]. Accessed at https://ednote.ecs.org/perkins-v-expanding-opportunities-for-work -based-learning on July 31, 2019.

Weedmark, D. (n.d.). *What are values in a workplace?* Accessed at https://work.chron.com/values -workplace-29708.html on November 5, 2020.

Wilson, C. (2010). *Bruce Tuckman's forming, storming, norming & performing team development model.* Accessed at http://sst7.org/media/BruceTuckman_Team_Development_Model.pdf on December 8, 2020.

Wisconsin Department of Public Instruction. (2015, May). *Career and technical education.* Accessed at https://dpi.wi.gov/cte on July 18, 2019.

Workforce Solutions. (n.d.). *When I grow up: Career lessons and activities for grades 9–12.* Accessed at www.wrksolutions.com/Documents/WhenIGrowUp/WIGU_PDFS/High-School/WFS-WIGU -HighSchool-Lessons.pdf on July 16, 2020.

World Economic Forum. (2016, January). *The future of jobs: Employment, skills and workforce strategy for the Fourth Industrial Revolution.* Geneva, Switzerland: Author. Accessed at http://www3.we forum.org/docs/WEF_Future_of_Jobs.pdf on August 2, 2019.

World Economic Forum. (2020a, January). *Jobs of tomorrow: Mapping opportunity in the new economy.* Geneva, Switzerland: Author. Accessed at www.weforum.org/reports/jobs-of-tomorrow -mapping-opportunity-in-the-new-economy on February 10, 2020.

World Economic Forum. (2020b, October). *The future of jobs report 2020.* Geneva, Switzerland: Author. Accessed at http://www3.weforum.org/docs/WEF_Future_of_Jobs_2020.pdf on November 1, 2020.

Yeager, D. S., Hanselman, P., Walton, G. M., Murray, J. S., Crosnoe, R., Muller, C., et al. (2019). A national experiment reveals where a growth mindset improves achievement. *Nature 573*, 364– 369. Accessed at www.nature.com/articles/s41586-019-1466-y on November 6. 2020.

Youth Service America. (n.d.). *Semester of service teacher toolkit.* Accessed at https://leadasap.ysa.org /wp-content/uploads/2017/10/Semester-of-Service-Teacher-Toolkit.pdf on January 12, 2020.

Zalis, S. (2017, November 30). *The truth about diversity—and why it matters.* Accessed at www.forbes .com/sites/shelleyzalis/2017/11/30/the-truth-about-diversity-and-why-it-matters/?sh=386603666e71 on November 3, 2020.

Index

Ready for Anything
Suzette Lovely
Effective teaching and learning must reflect what's happening technologically, socially, economically, and globally. In *Ready for Anything*, author Suzette Lovely introduces four touchstones that will invigorate students' curiosity and aspirations and prepare them for college, careers, and life in the 21st century.
BKF848

Growing Tomorrow's Citizens in Today's Classrooms
Cassandra Erkens, Tom Schimmer, and Nicole Dimich
For students to succeed in today's ever-changing world, they must acquire unique knowledge and skills. Practical and research-based, this resource will help educators design assessment and instruction to ensure students master critical competencies, including collaboration, critical thinking, creative thinking, communication, digital citizenship, and more.
BKF765

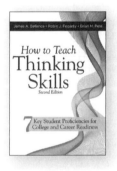

How to Teach Thinking Skills, Second Edition
James A. Bellanca, Robin J. Fogarty, and Brian M. Pete
Ensure your students develop the higher-order, complex thinking skills they need to not just survive but thrive in a 21st century world. The latest edition of this best-selling guide details a practical, three-phase teaching model and dives deep into seven essential student proficiencies.
BKF900

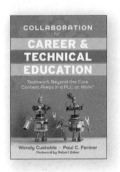

Collaboration for Career and Technical Education
Wendy Custable and Paul C. Farmer
All teachers—including career and technical education (CTE) teachers—play a vital role in building a thriving PLC. In this practical resource, the authors explicitly outline how CTE educators can integrate PLC best practices and collaborative team processes into their daily work.
BKF940

Solution Tree | Press
a division of

Solution Tree

Visit SolutionTree.com or call 800.733.6786 to order.

Wait! Your professional development journey doesn't have to end with the last pages of this book.

We realize improving student learning doesn't happen overnight. And your school or district shouldn't be left to puzzle out all the details of this process alone.

No matter where you are on the journey, we're committed to helping you get to the next stage.

Take advantage of everything from **custom workshops** to **keynote presentations** and **interactive web and video conferencing**. We can even help you develop an action plan tailored to fit your specific needs.

Let's get the conversation started.

Call 888.763.9045 today.

SolutionTree.com